CURRIER AND IVES

THE ROAD,—WINTER.

PUBLISHED BY N. CURRIER, 152 NASSAU ST. NEW YORK.

PLATE 1

G. H. Durrie
1856

HOME TO THANKSGIVING.

NEW YORK. PUBLISHED BY CURRIER & IVES, 152 NASSAU STREET.

PLATE 2

CURRIER & IVES

Printmakers to the American People

BY

HARRY T. PETERS

DOUBLEDAY, DORAN & CO., INC.

Garden City, New York

MCMXLIII

THIS SPECIAL EDITION OF
CURRIER & IVES
IS SET IN 12 PT. CASLON MONOTYPE
WITH HAND-DRAWN DECORATIVE INITIALS
THE DESIGN AND TYPOGRAPHY IS BY
A. P. TEDESCO
AND THE BOOK HAS BEEN PRODUCED
BY ZEESE-WILKINSON COMPANY, INC.
AND H. WOLFF BOOK MANUFACTURING COMPANY

DEDICATED
TO THE MEMORY OF THOSE RESOLUTE AMERICANS
WHOSE STURDY ACHIEVEMENTS IN BUILDING AN EMPIRE
PROVIDED INSPIRATION FOR THE PRINTS IN
THE CURRIER & IVES GALLERY

CONTENTS

ILLUSTRATIONS

Asterisks denote plates in full color.

[xv]

CURRIER AND IVES

CENTRAL-PARK, WINTER.
THE SKATING POND.

Plate 3

THE LIFE OF A FIREMAN.

The Metropolitan System.

PLATE 4

I. COLORED ENGRAVINGS FOR THE PEOPLE

ON THE EVENING of January 13, 1840, the steamboat *Lexington*, bound from New York for Stonington, Connecticut, with a crew of forty and nearly one hundred passengers, caught fire on Long Island Sound. The wooden vessel burned like tinder, the lifeboats, badly handled, capsized on being launched, and the pilot's effort to run the ship ashore failed when the engines stopped two miles from the coast. Occupants of the vessel had to choose between burning to death and drowning in the frigid water. Only a handful survived.

Three days later, when New York was still humming with conflicting tales of the disaster, there appeared what was perhaps the first illustrated extra in history. Headed "The Extra Sun," it bears a finely drawn and violently realistic picture of the flaming vessel. Figures can be seen lining the rails fore and aft and leaping into the water while a starboard lifeboat spills its occupants into the sea after a clumsy launching. In the foreground frenzied women and men in stovepipe hats take a precarious refuge on the cotton bales that were the ship's chief cargo and cling desperately to bits of debris. The print, which is followed by seven solid columns of letterpress describing the holocaust, is captioned "Awful Conflagration of the Steam Boat 'Lexington' in Long Island Sound on Monday Eveg. Jany. 13th 1840, by which melancholy occurrence over 100 persons perished." In small letters at the lower left-hand corner of the print are the words "Drawn by W. K. Hewitt," and at the right, "N. Currier, Lith. & Pub. 2 Spruce St. N. Y."

"The Extra Sun" was a sensation. It received columns of newspaper notices. Newsboys hawked it in the streets. The presses ran night and day to supply the demand. Copies were shipped to other cities, and overnight N. Currier became a national institution.

[1]

The *Lexington* print, the first great Currier best seller, is typical of the work of a firm that for over fifty years combined artistic talent, skilled craftsmanship, and merchandising acumen with the keenest news sense of the day. It revealed the tremendous sales potentialities of newsworthy pictures at a time when the various processes now in common use for the swift and accurate reproduction of drawings and photographs were mostly unknown. For the youthful firm of N. Currier it opened up a new line of "rush stock," depicting events and persons in the news, a line which, with the small "stock prints," was to prove its chief source of income. It launched the firm on a half-century of prosperity as "Printmakers to the American People," during which time it depicted with fidelity and endless imagination every phase of life in a country that was growing from adolescence to maturity.

In 1834, when Nathaniel Currier formed his first partnership, Andrew Jackson was President, the South was a slaveholding oligarchy, Texas still belonged to Mexico, the Great West was a wilderness, and the industrial revolution had yet to penetrate what was still an agricultural nation. In 1888, when Currier died, he left a country spanned from coast to coast by the railroads that had been only a curious experiment in 1834; a country which had fought a desperate war to preserve its unity and which had emerged from that war into a period of expansion and industrial growth unprecedented in history. His lifetime covered the conquest of the West, the harnessing of steam, the rise of industrialism, the Civil War and its aftermath of reconstruction and unification. They were years that saw an uncertain young republic establish itself as a great Power, the formative years of a great nation, years crowded with events that cried for accurate and graphic presentation to a public that was becoming increasingly alive to the tempo of the times. Such a presentation the firms of N. Currier and later Currier & Ives were to provide generously in the form of inexpensive, finely executed lithographic prints that made their way into nearly every home and became in an amazingly short time an American institution.

The Currier & Ives prints covered a wide variety of subject matter, from comics to reproductions of oil paintings by the finest artists of the day, from sentimental scenes to portraits of the great. There were prints of disasters and wrecks, of Mexican and Civil War land and naval battles, of clipper ships and whalers, of railroads and fire scenes. There were political cartoons and campaign banners; portraits of presidents, pugilists, and of such notables as General Tom Thumb; panoramic views of cities and scenes of farm and country life; scenes that depicted the winning of the West and life among the Indians; sporting prints, hunting and fishing pictures; a gallery of prints that helped immortalize the American trotter; and prints with a hundred other subjects as varied and as colorful as America itself.

The entire collection of the seven thousand or more prints that are now known forms a great panoramic picture of mid-nineteenth-century America. No era of history has been more fortunate in its portrayers. Currier & Ives pictured their own times with meticulous accuracy of detail, without "artiness," and with no thought of appealing to any but their own immediate market. They gave the public pictures that were easy to understand and appreciate, pictures that were typically American, and pictures not only with subjects that were within the knowledge and experience of the average man but at prices that were within the range of his pocketbook. Currier & Ives, who styled themselves simply as publishers of "Colored Engravings for the People," were a democratic firm in a democratic country. In their methods of production and distribution they were decades ahead of their times. In their heyday Currier prints were to be found adorning the walls of barrooms, barbershops, firehouses, and hotels, as well as of the homes of rich and poor alike.

Today the same prints that were sold by the thousands for five to twenty-five cents apiece and never for more than three dollars apiece (this for the large folios) are collectors' items. They are eagerly sought out in print shops and at auctions and bring prices that range all the way from a few dollars for some of the smaller and commoner prints to the record three thousand dollars paid for a large folio print in 1928. The reasons for their disappearance and for their skyrocketing in value in so comparatively short a time are easy to understand. In the latter part of the last century came the development of chromolithography, photography, and photoengraving; newspapers and illustrated weeklies began to take a prominent place in American life. With their rise the hand-colored lithographs of Currier & Ives began to go out of vogue. Because they had cost little they were not greatly cherished when newer and more fashionable pictures took their places on the walls. Thousands must have been destroyed and discarded as valueless.

Now with the perspective that the passage of half a century or so has given us we can see their value and their merit. Some are crude, it is true, but more are the work of accomplished and talented artists. Some are merely quaint, some mawkishly sentimental and moralistic, and in some melodrama passes for drama. But more have distinction of line and composition, gracious coloring, and conscientious attention to accuracy of detail. All are homely in the best sense; simple, sincere representations of an era that is past. They belong to the genus Americanus and embody so genuine a record of our development and culture that the permanence of their place is assured.

Some knowledge of the process by which the Currier & Ives prints were reproduced, of the backgrounds of Nathaniel Currier and James Merritt Ives, of the workings of their busy shop, and of the artists and lithographers employed there is necessary for a complete understanding and appreciation of the prints themselves. For the story of the firm, of its men and its methods, is nearly as unique and revealing as the pictures it produced.

II. MR. CURRIER
AND MR. IVES

IN THE EARLY nineteenth century, when pictures in books and magazines were reproduced only by relatively slow and cumbersome processes—from copperplate engravings, from woodcuts, or by some similar method—engravers and publishers in Europe and in America were beginning to experiment with a new and simpler invention. This new process was called lithography (meaning "writing on stone"), and it depended on so simple a principle as the natural antipathy between grease and water.

Lithography had been invented around 1795 by a Bavarian named Alois Senefelder. It was introduced in France in 1816 and was being used successfully in London in 1822. Meanwhile this ingenious new idea had already reached the United States, where in 1819 or 1820 the painter Bass Otis, a pupil of Gilbert Stuart, was making the first American experiments.

Senefelder's invention, like many other brilliant ones, was remarkably simple. It demanded first of all a special kind of soft and very porous stone. The stones used by Currier & Ives were of calcareous slate, imported from Solenhofen, Bavaria, and bought and sold by the pound. The stone was cut in flat rectangular blocks to the required length and width and a couple of inches in thickness. A soft yellowish gray in color, the stone was then prepared for the lithographer by grinding. A very thin layer of sand was spread over it, and it was ground smooth by another stone rubbed over it with a circular motion. This process, known as "graining," gave the stone a fine, velvety surface texture, so delicate that a touch of the fingers could damage it.

The stone was now ready for the design, which would be sketched on it with special lithographic crayons made of water-repelling substances. The crayons varied in width from

[4]

the delicate "diamond" size, used for lettering, to coarser grades one and a half inches wide. As the design was worked on the stone the crayons were supplemented with brushes and with an alpaca pad for shading. The work was extremely delicate and required precision and faultless accuracy, for no erasure was possible. A line could be removed, but no proper line could be put in its place without regraining the stone.

The stone, with the complete design now sketched on it, was given a bath of gum and acids. Those parts of the stone not protected by the crayon would bubble up under the acid, and when the stone had been washed clean with another solution the crayon design, hardy enough to resist the acid, would stand out in low relief. The stone was now a plate ready for printing.

The plate was now wet thoroughly, the water being absorbed by the porous exposed stone and repelled by the parts covered with crayon. With the plate placed in the press a special greasy ink was applied to the roller. An original Currier & Ives formula for the making of lithographic ink that has come down to us shows it to be a curious substance, compounded of beef suet, goose grease, white wax, castile soap, gum mastic, shellac, and gas black. As the roller passed over the plate the greasy ink was picked up by the crayon and repelled by the wet stone. The paper could then be placed on the inked plate, pressure applied and released, and a print "pulled" from the press. In the Currier & Ives shop the print would then be ready for coloring by hand.

The first American firm to make a commercial success of lithography was William S. & John Pendleton of Boston. Establishing their business in 1824, the Pendletons in 1825 brought from France a man named Dubois who was the first true lithographic pressman in America. By 1828 the business had grown to the point where it was necessary to hire an apprentice. The job was given to a fifteen-year-old boy named Nathaniel Currier.

Thus Nathaniel Currier had an early start in an infant business, and he was quick to master its intricacies and to realize its potentialities. After five years with the Pendletons the twenty-year-old Currier went to Philadelphia to work with a master lithographer, M. E. D. Brown. A year later he came to New York, where he and John Pendleton had planned to start a business of their own. However, Pendleton, arriving in New York first, received another offer so attractive that he could not refuse it, and he sold his share in the projected business to Currier, who entered into a partnership with a man named Stodart in 1834. This proved an unfortunate move, and the firm of Currier & Stodart survived for only a year. It apparently operated a job press, doing work on commission rather than original publishing of prints. That Currier, however, considered this his start in the business is evident from the fact that subsequent N. Currier and Currier & Ives letterheads bore the legend "Founded in 1834."

The unsuccessful partnership dissolved, Nathaniel Currier, at twenty-two, established his own business at 1 Wall Street in 1835. In 1836 Currier moved his office to Nassau Street and two years later found it necessary to establish the "factory" at 2 Spruce Street, with 152 Nassau devoted entirely to the store. Years later the factory was located at 33 Spruce Street.

There is little definite record of Currier's work in 1834 and 1835. Many catalogues and collectors have placed certain prints as Currier's made before 1835, but the best authenticated opinion seems to agree that the earliest Currier print now known, of the type that made them famous, is "Ruins of the Planters Hotel, New-Orleans, Which fell at two O'clock, on the Morning of the 15th of May 1835, burying 50 persons, 40 of which escaped with their Lives. Printed by N. Currier 1 Wall St. N. York. On Stone by J. H. Bufford" (84). This print, which differs somewhat in composition and style from most prints generally known to collectors as Currier & Ives, is also unusual in its size (7½ in. × 9 in.) and in the fact that it is uncolored. Another early print, which indeed may be the first, is "Ruins of the Merchant's Exchange N.Y. After the Destructive Conflagration of Decbr. 16 & 17, 1835. Sketched and drawn on Stone by J. H. Bufford" (84). Directly under the print, within the plate line, appears "N. Currier's Press." This print is also uncolored. It will be readily seen that Nathaniel Currier was aware of the commercial possibilities of fire and disaster pictures well before the famous *Lexington* print appeared.

There is a portrait, dated 1834, of William P. Dewees, professor of obstetrics at the University of Pennsylvania, from the painting by John Neagle and done on stone by Currier's former associate, M. E. D. Brown. This print, as finely executed as any of the firm's later work, bears the imprint, "N. Currier's Press." Perhaps the earliest in color is the one of "Upper Canada College, by J. H. Bufford on Stone" bearing the words, "N. Currier – Lith., N. Y.," and dated 1835. But both of these were probably only commission jobs and not a part of the firm's subsequent sale prints.

The first entry by N. Currier in the copyright records in Washington is under 1838, and the next in 1840. Undoubtedly during this early period Currier produced a number of prints that he did not copyright, his work not having become sufficiently popular to necessitate that precaution. Some collectors claim that a number of the undated and un-copyrighted smaller prints were made during this period.

City directories describe the firm variously as "Publishers," "Print Publishers," "Publishers of Prints and Engravings," and "Lithographers." Indeed Currier & Ives themselves seem to have had no fixed method of describing their firm's activities, although their designations were always as simple and unpretentious as was their work. An early card says, "N. Currier, Lithographer and Publisher." A card of the seventies and a letterhead of the eighties use the words "Currier & Ives, Publishers of Cheap and Popular Pictures." On another letterhead is the word "Printmakers." Perhaps the happiest of all is the ingenuous and charming phrase that was used first by Nathaniel Currier in the firm's early days: "Colored Engravings for the People" (5). The firm's success amply justified that title.

Nathaniel Currier, born in Roxbury, Massachusetts, in 1813, was a man of medium height, fair-complexioned and blue-eyed. He was gentlemanly and liberal and devoted to his business, which he conducted with enterprise and vigor. In ideas he was far ahead of his times. He had geniality and charm, fine critical artistic judgment, a remarkable aware-ness of public taste, and a shrewd business sense. His affable personality and keen sense of humor made him many friends, and his shop was a favorite resort of many prominent men, among them Henry Ward Beecher, Horace Greeley, and P. T. Barnum. Currier married twice and had one son, Edward West Currier, by his first wife, who had been Miss Eliza West of Boston. In 1847 he married a second time. His second wife, the former Miss Lura Ormsbee "of Vermont," bore him one son who died in infancy.

Currier had a summer home in Amesbury, Massachusetts, which he called "The Lion's Mouth." There he was visited often by the poet, John Greenleaf Whittier. He liked horses and kept a number of them at Amesbury. The well-known print, "The Road—Summer," published in 1853, is a portrait of the publisher's brother, Charles Currier, driving one of his horses at Amesbury, and "The Road,—Winter" (1) shows Currier and his wife driving in their sleigh. The latter print was produced and presented to Currier by his employees. He was so delighted with it that he added it to the list as a stock item.

For many years Nathaniel Currier had his brother Charles as a business associate. Five years Nathaniel's junior, Charles had desk space at the factory. He took orders for the firm on commission and also ran a quite separate business of his own. In an advertisement in the New York City Directory of 1862 he describes himself as: "Charles Currier: Lithographer, 33 Spruce Street. Portraits, views of cities, towns and buildings, book illustrations, maps and circulars, show cards in colors or plain, music titles, bill-heads, etc., executed in the first style of the art; also manufacturer of lithographic crayons superior to any others."

That final claim was no idle boast and reveals by far the most important part of his work. With the assistance of one of the Currier & Ives artists, Mrs. Fanny Palmer, Charles invented a lithographic crayon far superior to the French crayons formerly used. We have the word of another Currier & Ives artist and lithographer, Louis Maurer, that these crayons were beyond question the best ever made for the purpose. Charles Currier manufactured them himself at the Spruce Street address and later in the attic of his Brooklyn home. As Maurer remembers it, the crayons were made of wax, soap, shellac, and other water-repelling substances. After their invention no other crayon was used at the Currier & Ives establishment.

Charles apparently lacked much of the ambition and application by which his brother reached the top of his profession and achieved fame. He worked by fits and starts, was generally well behind in his orders for the crayons, and failed to build up the business to anything like its potentialities. Short and somewhat plump, wearing side whiskers and a beard but no mustache, and addicted to a tall white hat, Charles was a distinct individual.

Oddly enough it was he who had what was apparently the only complete file of all the lithographs made by N. Currier and Currier & Ives up to about 1880. These were all proof prints and were contained in three large cases. They were taken from the Spruce Street office to Charles's home, where for lack of space they were placed under the entrance stoop. When Charles moved to Brooklyn the cases went along but were consigned to a damp cellar. After their owner's death the cases were opened and it was found that nearly all the prints had been destroyed by dampness and exposure. Only a few at the bottom of each case were worth saving. These were given away and otherwise scattered. It is probably typical of Charles's easygoing and careless nature that such a collection, which, sold intact at 1928 prices, would have realized a sizable fortune, should receive such treatment.

As indicated by his advertisement, Charles Currier also did some print publishing under his own name. He occupied the 33 Spruce Street address before his brother moved his factory there. Among the prints that bear the C. Currier imprint are "Soldier's Return" (7), "Permanent Fair Grounds of the Queens County Agricultural Society" (169), and "Birds Eye View of Mt. Vernon, the Home of Washington" (179). Apparently Charles worked about in the shop and store at what interested him, presented ideas for stones to the firm, and perhaps if they were not accepted made them himself.

Besides his invention of the superior lithographic crayon, Charles made another invaluable contribution to his brother's firm. His wife's sister had married a young bookkeeper, art lover, and lithographer whom Charles recommended to Nathaniel for a position. In 1852 the young man was hired as a bookkeeper. He fitted so well into the rapidly expanding firm that five years later he was made a partner. His name was James Merritt Ives.

Ives turned out to be an ideal partner for Nathaniel Currier. He had a solid grounding in business methods and soon assumed the position of general manager of the firm. But his contribution was far more extensive than a simple establishment of the firm as financially stable and profitable. He had long been an enthusiastic art lover, a frequent visitor to galleries and exhibits and to the Astor Library. In addition he was a self-educated artist of no mean ability.

The new partner showed himself to be unusually adept in showing how an idea could be used to best advantage. His criticism of sketches was keen, and he was clever at combining features from various sketches into a well-designed composite whole. This was a frequent Currier & Ives device, many of the prints being the work of more than one artist. Thomas Worth, the famous cartoonist, has said that he soon learned, when he began submitting his drawings to the firm, that Ives had quite as much to say about whether a picture should be accepted as did Currier. The junior partner, too, had a sure sense for what would be popular and salable.

When he joined the firm in 1852 Ives was twenty-eight years old, eleven years younger than his employer. He was born in a cottage on the grounds of Bellevue Hospital, of which his father was superintendent. At twelve he was sent downtown to work. He pursued his work and his avocation of learning about artists and art with characteristic vigor. He learned lithography and after entering Currier's employ occasionally worked on stones himself. His work on the fourth plate of the delightful folio series, "The Four Seasons of Life," reveals his skillful draftsmanship. "Old Age. 'The Season of Rest'" (107), the fourth plate in the series, is reproduced here.

Ives's life was regular, prosperous, and happy. He had a large family—two sons and four daughters. His interests were many and varied. He was a religious man and also took an active part in politics and in civic welfare work. His knowledge and appreciation of art were recognized in artistic circles outside of the business, and he served on many committees and boards that awarded prizes.

Thomas Worth has described him as "a very short and dumpy little man, thickset and just the opposite of his partner." He appealed to Worth especially because his sense of humor was keen. He could see the point of a cartoon without hunting for it. Worth found him a congenial companion when they visited the various trotting tracks to make sketches of the horses for future prints. These excursions must have been among Ives pleasantest duties in connection with the company, for, like Currier, he was very fond of horses. He always kept one or two well-bred, fast driving horses, and the trotting and other horse prints were his favorites.

The only interruption in his work with the firm after he joined it in 1852 was his period of service with the Union forces during the Civil War. Since he was nearly forty and married when the war broke out, he could very likely have avoided serving altogether without a question as to the sincerity of his patriotism. However, he organized and served as captain of F Company of the 23d Regiment, of Brooklyn, which saw active service during the Confederate invasion of Pennsylvania.

This likable and able man fitted so remarkably well into the business of N. Currier that it is not surprising that in a short five years he should be made a partner. His talents were in many ways complementary to those of Currier, and in the backgrounds and interests of the two men there was enough in common to make their association pleasant as well as successful. Successful it certainly was; Currier & Ives at their peak so far outstripped their competitors as to leave them virtually forgotten while they themselves quite unwittingly gained a fame that was not alone for their own time.

III. PRINTS AT SIX CENTS APIECE WHOLESALE

ROM 1838 to 1872 the N. Currier and Currier & Ives store was located at 152 Nassau Street. It must have been a delightful and, from the viewpoint of today's collector, a fabulous place. Thousands of prints that today would be worth many more thousands of dollars were stacked high on the tables, were pinned or tacked on the walls, and stood, framed and unframed, on display racks. Outside, when the weather was clear, tables piled with the cheaper prints stood on the sidewalk, guarded and sold by a boy.

The store had a frontage of about twenty-five feet and a depth of approximately seventy-five. The fifteen feet in the back served in the early days as the office and was fenced off by Currier's large standing desk, from which he supervised the store. The walls of the store were lined with great bins that contained the prints. Thick sheets of cardboard separated the various classes of subject, and the lid of each bin bore an inventory. Each lid, when raised, was a picture rack upon which the prints could be exhibited. Down the center of the store were long tables, piled high. In addition to prints, oil paintings that had been reproduced were hung on the walls of the office and store. The paintings, too, were offered for sale. Other locations of the firm from 1872 on were: 125 Nassau Street, 123 Nassau Street, 115 Nassau Street, and 108 Fulton Street.

The chief salesman and general sales manager for more than forty years was Daniel W. Logan, Sr., who in his youth had been a sailor. He had an average force of about five clerks who waited on customers, packed and shipped the prints, and did the other necessary chores about the store.

Distribution was by no means limited to retail sale in the store. After the success of the *Lexington* disaster print a number of pushcart salesmen would appear every morning at the store and each would select prints that he thought would suit the potential customers in his particular area. These were piled neatly on the carts, and in addition each peddler was supplied with a few prints to be attached to the sides of his cart to attract customers. Each peddler left a deposit on the prints taken. At night the peddlers returned with the prints left, had their deposits refunded, and paid for the prints sold.

The appointment of regular agents and sale to less regular peddlers in other cities was the next step. Distribution was astonishingly wide. Dealers and collectors have found prints in every section of the country, giving evidence of the fact that Currier & Ives agents must have been many and active. The firm also had a London office. It was probably from this agency that the great mass of prints that has been found abroad was distributed. In France the comics and the clipper-ship prints were especially popular, while Germany and Great Britain preferred the views and Western scenes. The pictures in fact seem to have reached every part of Europe, which is not surprising in view of the fact that their subject matter was so varied as to appeal to every possible taste. They were also, of course, extremely cheap.

At wholesale the small prints sold for six cents apiece, six dollars a hundred, and sixty dollars a thousand. In the store the single prints were sold at from fifteen to twenty-five cents apiece, except those lots of remainders that were sold at the sidewalk tables at almost any price. The large folios, which were colored by outside artists or colorists, sold at retail from one dollar and fifty cents to three dollars each. There is no record of the wholesale prices of the large folios. The prints were issued in a variety of sizes, from the smallest, measuring about 2.8 inches × 4.8, to the "large folio" size, which measured about 18 × 27 inches.

Throughout its history the firm issued a number of large catalogues in which the available prints were listed, much in the same manner that book publishers issue "trade lists." There were also special catalogues for some of the different groups of prints, like the celebrated fire pictures. Some of these catalogues have come down to us and have proved helpful to collectors and dealers in straightening out sets. They have also revealed titles of prints that have become lost altogether. An 1851 advertisement lists a large folio print of "The Celebrated Fighting Pig 'Pape,' weighing only 34 lbs. . . . representing him as he fought the 46½ lb Dog, 'Crib' on the evening of the 18th March, 1849." The print was found only a few years ago—of all places in California. The catalogues have also made clear the significance of the small italic numbers that appear at the bottom of many of the prints. These were the catalogue numbers apparently assigned for the convenience of dealers, who could order by number rather than by the often unwieldy titles.

In mailing catalogues to agents, Currier & Ives used accompanying sales letters, quite in the manner of our own time. An undated form letter of the seventies, entirely lithographed in a handsome, florid hand, is here transcribed:

New York. . . . . .187. . . .

Dear Sir,

Herewith we enclose our new Catalogue of Popular Cheap Prints containing nearly Eleven hundred subjects, from which you can make your own selection of kinds wanted. You will notice that the Catalogue comprises Juvenile, Domestic, Love Scenes, Kittens and Puppies, Ladies Heads, Catholic Religious, Patriotic, Landscapes, Vessels, Comic, School Rewards and Drawing Studies, Flowers and Fruits, Motto Cards, Horses, Family Registers, Memory Pieces and Miscellaneous in great variety, and all elegant and salable Pictures.

Our experience of over Thirty years in the Trade enables us to select for Publication, subjects best adapted to suit the popular taste, and to meet the wants of all sections, and our Prints have become a staple article which are in great demand in every part of the country.

To Peddlers or Travelling Agents, these Prints offer great inducements, as they are easily handled and carried, do not require a large outlay of money to stock up with, and afford a handsomer profit than almost any article they can deal in, while at the same time Pictures have now become a necessity, and the price at which they can be retailed is so low, that everybody can afford to buy them. . . .

Our terms are strictly Cash with the order and on receipt of same we carefully envelope and promptly forward prints the same day that the order is received. . . . Be careful to sign letter plainly with name of writer, Town, Country, and State; we are sometimes much troubled by receiving letters containing money without signature, or date of place whence mailed. Address letters plainly to

Currier & Ives
123 & 125 Nassau St.
New York

The letter is interesting in that it reveals the enormous number and variety of prints offered for sale and the fact that Currier & Ives appealed to "Peddlers or Travelling Agents" as well as to permanent representatives in other cities. Also it will be noted that the firm, after many years of business, adhered strictly to the cash method.

The factory at 33 Spruce Street was a five-story building, the basement and first two floors of which were rented out. Here, from 1866 to 1907, when the firm was finally liquidated, the prints of Currier & Ives were produced. The walls of the upper three floors were lined with racks for the stones, which were numbered on the ends for ready use. The grinding and regrinding of the stones was a full-time job at which a man on the fourth floor worked steadily. The stones of the best-selling prints were often kept standing, while those of less successful pictures were reground after the first editions. When a demand arose for a print the stone of which had been reground, the print would be relithographed. This accounts for the several states of some of the prints. On a "rush print" on which there was an unusually heavy immediate sale it was sometimes necessary to lithograph the same design on several stones and print from all at once. This also accounts for variations.

The fourth floor rear was reserved for the artists, lithographers, and letterers. Many of the prints were, of course, the work of artists who worked outside the Currier & Ives shop. There were, however, a number of accomplished artists like Louis Maurer and Mrs. Fanny Palmer who for varying periods cf time were in the firm's regular employ. Maurer was also an expert lithographer. The other principal lithographers were Otto Knirsch,

Franz Venino, John Cameron, C. Severin, J. Schultz, and Napoleon Sarony, the latter also an artist of considerable ability.

For a number of years Otto Knirsch worked for himself and sold the finished stones to Currier & Ives. Independent lithographers like Knirsch were paid forty or fifty dollars for finished stones for the smaller prints. The fastest and most prolific workman in the firm's own group was Franz Venino, a German-Italian who was a pupil of the great Kaulbach. Heads, faces, and cartoons were his specialty. He was without imagination but was an extremely able draftsman once he was given an idea. He could turn out one of the small plates a week and sometimes even more. Benino designed as well as lithographed a number of the women's heads and had an indeterminate part in the production of the many "sentimentals." Severin, another very skillful craftsman, took occasional jobs and finished them in his own good time, getting paid for specific work. He lithographed the famous trotting-horse print, "Peytona and Fashion" (9), today among the most valuable of all the Currier & Ives gallery, and also "Husking" (49), the only work of the painter Eastman Johnson that Currier & Ives reproduced and among the very finest of their prints. Practically all the lettering during the greater part of the firm's history was done by J. Schultz.

Like Schultz and Franz Venino, John Cameron was a regular Currier & Ives employee over a long period of years. He was a hunchback and had a fondness for drink, but his work was of very high quality and his output very large. Even after ill health confined him to his home on Long Island, stones were sent out for him to work on there. Although his name appears as artist of some of the jointly designed prints, he was only a lithographer. There is evidence that he lithographed the Thomas Worth cartoons, often working from very crude sketches. Perhaps his most important contribution was his work on the horse prints, which establishes him in the first rank. Cameron's best work is demonstrated in his noble print, "Imported Messenger" (184), showing one of the great forbears of our modern race horse.

Napoleon Sarony achieved his fame in activities other than his work for Currier & Ives, but early in his career he was employed as a lithographer by Nathaniel Currier. His was a master hand, and as a lithographer he had few equals. Much of his work was unsigned, but because of his superior craftsmanship many of the Sarony prints are easily recognizable. Born in Quebec in 1821 of French-Austrian extraction, Sarony was a colorful character. He lived well and traveled extensively, making and spending several fortunes during a full life. Sarony's interests were amazingly wide. His black-and-white drawings were exhibited in the National Academy in New York and in London galleries. He was also perhaps the most successful of all the early experimenters with photography, developing as he did the fashionable cabinet-size photograph of those days. With H. B. Major, who had also served a period of apprenticeship with Currier, Sarony set up the lithographing firm of Sarony & Major. Although the new firm was in a sense a competitor of Currier & Ives, the two companies actually worked in harmony and often helped each other. Famous lithographers like Maurer and Severin worked for both firms at one time or another, and when Sarony & Major went out of business Currier & Ives bought all their plates and later used some of them. Nevertheless, had Sarony remained in the employ of Currier & Ives it is certain that the story of the firm would have been quite different. He would have introduced more modern methods, and Currier & Ives would not have continued to the end of their career making prints by the old single-stone hand-colored process.

Sarony's most important work for Currier was the famous *Lexington* print, which he designed. This print was issued in a second state after the huge initial demand had slackened. The second state (21) omits the heading, "The Extra Sun," and has a new text—the testimony of Captain Hilliard, one of the few survivors of the disaster. Sarony contributed much of the work on a long line of posters known as Barnum's Gallery of Wonders; he was responsible for the prints of the ox-eyed beauties who appeared in a series of pictures of named women; and finally he produced a number of the best naval prints issued by Currier & Ives.

No definite information is available on how the Currier & Ives prints were signed, and no consistent method seems to have been used. Sometimes the artist's name appears, but often only the lithographer's, and in many cases there is no signature at all. It is therefore often impossible to attribute work to specific individuals.

On the Spruce Street side of the third and fourth floors of the factory were the presses. These were all hand-operated and were so situated because the printers required good light.

The fifth floor was given over to the colorists. It has come as a surprise to many dealers and collectors to learn that all Currier & Ives prints were hand-colored. They were neither lithographed in color nor printed in color, but lithographed and printed in one-color ink and colored by hand afterward.

Chromolithography, whereby pictures were reproduced in color from stones, one color from a stone, was not used in this country before 1860. The chromolithographs first introduced here did not have subjects of great American interest and were sold at rather high prices. The first Currier & Ives chromo, reproduced from an oil painting by Louis Maurer, was published in 1889, near the end of the firm's life. It was entitled "The Futurity Race, Sheepshead Bay, 1888, Won by Proctor Knott." This and all the other true chromos produced by Currier & Ives were not made in their own shop, since they did not have the necessary equipment, but were sent out to other shops for execution. They cannot properly be included among the gallery of typical prints that made the firm famous. The word "chromo" was frequently misused, however, long before the true chromos had gained widespread popularity, and the hand-colored prints were sometimes mistakenly referred to as such.

In the Currier & Ives shop the stock prints were colored by a staff of about twelve young women, all trained colorists and mostly of German descent. They worked at long tables from a model set up in the middle of the table, where it was visible to all. The models, many of which were colored by Louis Maurer and Fanny Palmer, were all first approved by one of the partners. Each colorist applied only one color and, when she had finished, passed the print on to the next worker, and so on until it was fully colored. The print would then go to the woman in charge, known as the "finisher," who would touch it up where necessary. The colors used were imported from Austria and were the finest available, especially valued because they did not fade in the light.

When large numbers of the rush stock prints were needed, extra help was called in. Then stencils would be cut for the various colors and the extras would wash in the colors. The prints could then be touched up by the regular girls. The larger folios were sent out in lots with models to regular colorists who worked outside the shop. Usually twelve prints from one of the large folio plates were sent out at a time. These outside colorists were often indigent young artists who earned a modest living at this kind of work while awaiting the recognition of their own work. The pay was surely modest enough. Currier & Ives paid one cent apiece to colorists for the small prints, and one dollar for coloring twelve of the large folios.

There survives a bill dated December 12, 1840, from James Baillie to Currier for coloring 2,378 of the small prints. The bill, carefully itemized, and including $5.94 for materials, comes to $29.72, from which is deducted $10.08 that has apparently been paid Baillie on account. The note that the colorist appends to his bill is affecting: "N.B. I have included all I have on hand as they will be finished this evening——Please let me have all the prints you can muster, so as to be prepared for Monday." The prints that Baillie had colored were chiefly the religious stock items and patriotic pictures, but included also were four hundred of the sentimental print, "The Sailors Adieu" (6), and 125 of the *Lexington* disaster print. It is interesting to note that this latter print was still in active demand eleven months after the event.

Many prints were also available uncolored. These were often used in schools where the pupils colored them. Unfortunately many of them have also been colored in recent years and sold as originals. The trained eye, however, can readily detect modern coloring.

The models for coloring are most interesting. Several of them are in existence, having been salvaged at the remainder sale of the firm in 1907. They reveal clearly not only the method by which the prints were colored but also how closely both partners worked with the artists, lithographers, and colorists. On the margin of the model for the trotting-horse print, "Sontag and Flora Temple," appear, in the handwriting of one of the partners, the words: "Keep this pattern. Figures are right. Tone Flora down a little. Sky will do . . ." Marginal notes on the model for "Tacony and Mac" read: "Change vest and cap of rider on Tacony to carmine. Brighten up saddle cloths, print too dull. . . . More blue in sky. Get more green in grass. Put more tail on Mac. . . . Rush out ten copies."

Notes on some of the original drawings for the Thomas Worth cartoons are enlightening too. The original (24) of "A Mule Team on an Up Grade" (25) bears the following on the left-hand margin: "Mr. Cameron: Let the woman's foot come between the mule's forefoot so as to show his brace against her better. The child is meant to be wrapped up in a mattress. You need not put words 'To Kansas' on the rock." Here is proof beyond doubt that Cameron redid the Worth comics for the stone. On the original (24) of the companion print, "A Mule Team on a Down Grade" (25), is the note: "Mr. Cameron: the mule ought to be a trifle bigger, and the child grabbing the woman with one hand. Please preserve the facial expression of the mule which 'means business.' . . ."

Again, on the margins of the wash drawing (22) for the comic, "A Howling Swell—With His Scalp in Danger" (23), the following notes appear: "Taking the paleface medicine. Make the fellow a little more in the foreground and larger. Don't put in this Indian drunk, leave him out entirely." Cameron followed the instructions. The drunken Indian on the ground at the left of the drawing does not appear in the finished print.

On occasion a print would be found to be unsatisfactory after it had been lithographed. Then, after a few copies had been pulled off, the print would be studied and the desired changes indicated on it. It would then of course be necessary to relithograph the whole. This apparently was done in the case of the print "The Celebrated Horse Dexter, 'The King of the Turf'" (61). A copy has been found in which the figure of the horse has been inked out and another, cut out of another copy, has been pasted over it. The position of legs, head, and tail has been changed, and the entire horse is placed differently on the plate. This reconstructed print must have been the lithographer's final model, for it is exactly like the finished print.

The firm of Currier & Ives had a flourishing career as "The Grand Central Depot for Cheap and Popular Pictures," to quote one of their letterheads, until well after 1880. They were not without rivals. There were a score of firms engaged in the same or similar businesses over the years—Sarony & Major, Duval, Nagel & Weingaertner, C. B. & E. C. Kellogg, Thomas Kelly, J. Baillie, O. Knirsch, Lane & Scott, Haskell & Allen, Biddle, to mention only a few. Many of these men either got their start or worked in one capacity or another with N. Currier and Currier & Ives. Sarony, Major, and Knirsch have already been mentioned. J. Baillie, as has been noted, did outside coloring for Currier in the 1840s, collecting his cent apiece for the small prints. John W. A. Scott, of Lane & Scott, had been an apprentice with Nathaniel Currier in the shop of William S. and John Pendleton in Boston.

The output of these rival firms was not inconsiderable. In most cases the process and business methods used were much the same as those used by Currier & Ives. Few of the firms, however, published many of the large folio prints of the type of the finest Currier & Ives work that to date have been the most eagerly sought after by collectors. Many of the prints from competing houses do have historical, sentimental, or esthetic values, and there is a field there for collectors. The fact remains that none of these houses, or indeed not all of them together, had a list that could be compared either in variety of subject or in quality of workmanship with that of Currier & Ives. Sales catalogues of the twenties, the bonanza years for lithograph sales and prices, reveal that of all the old American lithographs sold publicly over a five-year period about 80 per cent were Currier & Ives prints.

In the last decades of the nineteenth century, as the original partners turned over the business to their sons, the firm of Currier & Ives changed little. Its methods and its stock were for the most part those originated in the fertile brains of Nat Currier and James Ives. The firm experimented somewhat tentatively with chromolithography, but, as has been pointed out, lacked the equipment to do this work in its own shop. Possibly there was little profit in farming the work out to other shops. In one field the firm did do pioneer work in the eighties and nineties. It started a line of "Grand Illuminated Posters" (85) and announced that Currier & Ives were prepared to produce posters for any and all sporting occasions. Posters were made also for the American Tobacco Company. But this excursion into the advertising and poster fields was short-lived. It was the last flowering of the old firm.

Nathaniel Currier retired from the firm in 1880. Fifty-two of his sixty-seven years had been spent in the business of lithography, forty-six of them as his own boss. His final act was to make a handsome gift to every employee. Eight years later he died of heart trouble at his home in New York.

Currier was succeeded in the firm by his son, Edward West Currier, a tall, gaunt, and dark-complexioned man who had studied law in a casual way before joining his father in business. Though his health was never robust he had worked as a salesman in the store and had learned the details of the business. He was genuinely interested in books, prints, and paintings, of which he had extensive collections. He remained a partner in the firm for twenty-two years after his father's retirement.

Charles Currier had died nearly two years before his brother, but James Ives remained active in the firm until shortly before his death in 1895. He too was succeeded by his son, Chauncey Ives, so that from 1895 to 1902 the firm was in the hands of the sons of the original partners. In 1902 the younger Currier sold out to Chauncey Ives, who gradually liquidated the business, finally selling out, in turn, five years later, to Daniel W. Logan, son of the former sales manager. By that time the firm occupied only one floor at 33 Spruce Street. Logan had planned to continue the business, but ill health forced him to abandon the idea. Finally, in 1907, he disposed of the remaining stock and equipment. The lithographic stones were sold by the pound, the drawings having been removed from all of them, save a set of the Thomas Worth Darktown Comics. These were sold, with reproduction rights, to another lithographic firm. Some of the "Darktown Fire Brigade" (133) prints were reissued under the imprint of Joseph Koehler. The prints at hand, being then thoroughly out of vogue and having not yet become desirable in the eyes of collectors, were sold at remainder prices. A fortune in prints must have passed through the hands of that 1907 auctioneer.

The development of new processes of picture reproduction and the rise of new mediums through which the public could be reached more simply and directly had left the old firm behind. The newspapers had taken over the job of informing the public about fires and disasters; photographs and drawings by popular artists in the illustrated weeklies had replaced the sentimental portraits of Currier & Ives on the walls of the average American home; chromolithographs were gaining in popularity over the more elaborate of the Currier & Ives large folio prints. A new century demanded a new outlook, and this the firm never acquired. Currier & Ives outlived their usefulness, and rather than reorganize the business along modern lines the sons preferred to accept the demise.

IV. THE ARTISTS

IT MAY SEEM STRANGE that in discussing the work of Currier & Ives so little has been said about the artists whose drawings and paintings the firm reproduced. In writing of almost any field of art the historian usually focuses his attention upon the life of the artist and upon the development of his work rather than upon its reception by the public or its commercial success or lack of it. Sale and distribution are minor factors compared to the importance of the work of art per se.

In the case of Currier & Ives the situation is almost reversed. They were quite candidly a commercial firm, "Publishers of Cheap and Popular Pictures," and little concerned with art in the strict sense of the word. The fact that they reproduced the work of many of the most prominent artists of the day was not the major factor in their success in their own time, nor indeed has it been of paramount importance in the revival of interest in their work in another age. They hired the best artists and the finest lithographers because, in the finest tradition of a period that had not learned the art of ballyhoo, they believed that the quality of their product would reflect itself in the commercial returns. Their appeal was to the masses with the cheaper prints, and to the middle classes with the more expensive ones. They were not aiming at a market that would be impressed by the names of artists. Their products had to sell themselves by the innate salability of their subject matter and by the quality of the workmanship, without benefit of the sales help of snob appeal. For the very reason that the appeal of the prints had perforce to be broad and general, they have become, for us, the most vivid representation of an era that could live otherwise only in the pages of history. Judged purely as art, little of the work of Currier & Ives would have lived; as a well-rounded, comprehensive, and truly representative picture of an age, all of it has lived and will live.

The primary interest, then, in Currier & Ives must naturally be in the firm itself; where its ideas originated, in the physical details of their execution, in how it reached its public. The artists must take second rank.

They surely did in the eyes of the firm. On a majority of the prints no artist's name appears. In many cases we can hazard a guess as to whose the work is, but in more the artist must remain anonymous. The firm had many sources of art work at its disposal. There were first of all the artists on its own staff like Louis Maurer and Fanny Palmer. They worked in the shop or went out on special assignments, Maurer often to the trotting tracks to draw the horses and Mrs. Palmer into the country to draw backgrounds for all manner of prints. There were the regular contributors like Thomas Worth who sold their drawings outright to the firm. A large number of the prints were copies of well-known paintings and line engravings, which, copyright protection being negligible, could be had for the lithographing. The long series, "A Midsummer Night's Dream," for instance, lithographed by Maurer, was taken, with changes, from popular English engravings of the time. Then, too, on almost any subject of current interest drawings were daily brought into the store and offered for sale. These were bought at anywhere from one to ten dollars apiece, in accordance with their quality. There was no question of royalties. The drawings were purchased outright, and the firm reserved the right to alter them in any way it saw fit. There were also independent lithographers, or perhaps men who worked for other firms, who would on occasion do a stone on their spare time and offer it, ready for printing, to Currier & Ives. A number of the small plates were bought in this way.

But although the supply of competent and even finished drawings undoubtedly exceeded the demand, Currier & Ives had many special jobs for which they sought out artists and commissioned them. Louis Maurer was once asked how the firm went about finding an artist for a particular job. "Well, if none of us could do it," he replied, "they would go and hold up Charlie Parsons [the famous Currier & Ives marine artist]. He knew everybody. Besides, there were large groups of young artists of all nationalities trying to make a living. Parsons could almost always get hold of someone to do almost anything." The commission jobs did not, however, go primarily to unknowns. Taking the large folio prints alone, a list of the artists would show a great preponderance of distinguished names, names of the leading artists of the period. These men and the artists who did the most important work on the smaller stock prints, where such credit can be assigned, deserve a special mention.

LOUIS MAURER

THE READER is already familiar with the name of Louis Maurer, which has appeared frequently in this chronicle. This grand old man, who lived a full century of energetic, active, and creative life, was the last survivor of the Currier & Ives old guard. He was actively associated with the firm for nearly a decade and in close touch with its work for fifty years. It is to him that we owe much of our knowledge of the actual workings of the shop and of the methods of the company. When he died in 1932 the last strand connecting our time with Currier's heyday was severed.

Maurer was a man of astonishing talents and energies, which indeed challenge credibility. His home on Forty-third Street, New York City, in which, he used to state with pride, he had lived for over sixty years, was filled with treasures and curios that could have found their place in any museum. In the lower part of the house was his collection of sea shells, beautiful even to the layman and marvelously displayed in cabinets made with his own hands. He himself had an expert's knowledge of conchology. In another room was his collection of flutes. He was an accomplished musician on this instrument and had given a number of recitals.

On the floor above were his gun cases, containing a remarkable collection of guns and rifles. As in the case of his other collections, this one was not the result of any lay or dilettante interest. He had been all his life a sharpshooter of renown and had a cabinet of medals and trophies attesting his skill. During the Civil War he was an instructor of marksmen at Palisades Park, New Jersey. At the age of ninety, in a championship match of his rifle club he filled the bull's-eye, without a single shot outside, making the only perfect score of the match.

When he was fifty, having already become a master of a half-dozen arts, proficiency in any one of which would have satisfied the average man, he decided to take up painting seriously. He became a pupil in the Gotham Art School. Later, at the National Academy of Design, he entered the class conducted by the late William Chase. Painting was his principal pastime during the latter half of his life.

Maurer was born in Germany, in Biebrich on the Rhine, in 1832, the eldest of five children. His father was a cabinetmaker. As a child Louis became proficient at drawing. At school he studied all branches of mechanical drawing, continuing these studies at a drawing school in Mainz. He developed a particular interest in anatomy and took special courses in the anatomy of animals, particularly of the horse.

The young Maurer wanted to become a painter, but the family's financial needs influenced him to turn to a more practical art. He was apprenticed to a lithographer and in a year and a half learned the making, retouching, and coloring of lithographs. He then turned his hand to ivory carving and, while mastering that art, also worked at home, assisting his father at the cabinetmaker's bench. He earned a good livelihood at his various trades.

In 1850 his family listened to the siren call of opportunity in America, and in July of the following year they set sail on a two-hundred-ton sailing vessel from Havre. After a fast passage of thirty-nine days the Maurers landed in New York. A week later Louis had borrowed tools from an acquaintance and gone to work as a wood carver. After three months, on the suggestion of a friend, he decided to investigate the opportunities in his old trade of lithography. Endicott & Company, where he first applied, had no place for him. Napoleon Sarony, to whom he went next, made the same reply. But his third attempt, with T. W. Strong on Nassau Street, was successful. He had been with Strong about six months when he met Charles Currier. Charles was impressed with Maurer's work and recommended that he go to see his brother, who he thought could offer him **a** better position. Maurer acted on this suggestion, taking along some samples of his work. Nat Currier liked what he saw and introduced the young lithographer to Ives, who even then engaged all the employees. Maurer was promptly put to work at a desk in the basement of 152 Nassau Street.

From 1852 to 1860 Louis Maurer worked continuously and exclusively for the firms of N. Currier and Currier & Ives. He was a valuable man to the firm because of the wide range of his talents. He could design, draw, and lithograph, and he was not limited to any particular type of subject. He excelled in the draftsmanship of figures and animals and had a keen sense of perspective. Some of the finest examples of Maurer's skillful drawing are the farm scene "Preparing for Market" (31), the intriguing print "The Rubber. 'Put to his Trumps'" (88), and the carefree carriage print "Out for a Days Shooting. Off for the Woods" (169). Perhaps his most important work for the firm was the famous series "The Life of a Fireman," a set of six exceptionally well executed large folios that had great popularity and that today are among the most eagerly sought-after prints in the Currier & Ives collection. The sixth of the series is "The Metropolitan System" (4), described in the Currier & Ives fire-picture catalogue as "spirited, stirring and lifelike." The graphic print "The American Fireman. Always Ready" (175), by Maurer, is a portrait of Nathaniel Currier himself dressed in a fireman's uniform.

Maurer's early studies of the anatomy of the horse stood him in good stead at Currier & Ives's. The credit for immortalizing in lithographic prints the American trotting horse should be assigned equally to Maurer, Thomas Worth, and John Cameron. Maurer's first horse print was "Flora Temple" (57). His picture of the immortal horse Lexington (184) is among the most famous of all the trotting prints. "'Trotting Cracks' on the Snow" (116), also by Maurer, typifies the early snow and ice racing indulged in with the American trotter.

Maurer's reminiscences of his work for Currier & Ives confirmed the belief of many experts that many of the prints were the product of a number of hands. He recalled that in some cases Fanny Palmer would do the backgrounds, he, under the direction of Ives, who was himself an artist, would design and draw in the figures, and Cameron would do the lithographing, not without adding a few touches to suit himself. The prevalence of this communal method, of course, makes it doubly difficult to attribute the unsigned prints to specific artists.

Another disconcerting piece of knowledge that Maurer revealed was the fact that neither he nor Arthur Fitzwilliam Tait, at the time that they were working on the American Indian prints, had any first-hand knowledge of Indians. Their research for the pictures was done in the Astor Library, where Ives took them to see Prince Maximilian of Wied's book on the Indian and its accompanying volume of illustrations by Bodmer. Maurer and Tait were also influenced by the vigorous and dramatic Western prints designed by the artist George Catlin. Two of Catlin's best prints that are reproduced here are "Buffalo Bull, Chasing Back. 'Turn About Is Fair Play'" (189) and "The Snow-Shoe Dance" (189). In later years Maurer himself made two extensive trips West, and his later painting reveals a thorough and intimate knowledge both of Indians and of the animals of the West.

At the outbreak of the Civil War Maurer wanted to marry a girl named Louisa Stein. He did not feel, however, that his income was adequate to support a family, so he asked the firm for a raise. The request was refused and Maurer began to look for a better-paying job. He found one with Major & Knapp, successors to Sarony & Major. The twenty-five-dollar-a-week salary that he received in this new position enabled him to marry.

Maurer received five dollars a week when he first went to work for Currier, but he recalled that later his pay was twelve dollars a week, then considered a good salary. He remembered too that once or twice Currier gave him raises voluntarily, but these increases could hardly have been substantial, since he left a congenial position in order to secure twenty-five dollars a week.

After he left the firm's employ he did considerable work for it on commission and lithographed many stones at home. He worked for Major & Knapp for some time, gradually getting into commercial work, and in 1872 formed a partnership with F. Heppenheimer. The house of Maurer & Heppenheimer was entirely a commercial one, making labels, show cards, letterheads, etc. It was a successful venture, so much so that Maurer was able to retire in 1884 with a comfortable income.

THOMAS WORTH

THE NAME OF Thomas Worth, like that of Maurer, has already made its appearance in these pages. He and Maurer alone of the group that contributed most to the success of Currier & Ives lived to see the rediscovered prints take their place as valued and sought-after collectors' items. Their rich reminiscences have provided us with much of what information we have of the workings of that busy shop.

A year or so younger than Louis Maurer, Thomas Worth was born and brought up in Greenwich Village, New York City. He began to draw at an early age. He was eighteen or twenty when he took his first sketch into the store of N. Currier. It was done on a piece of blue blotting paper and represented two boys driving an old gray horse harnessed to an old four-wheeled wagon. Dust was flying from a barrel of ashes on the back of the wagon, almost blinding the driver of another gray trotter, who was trying to pass the ash wagon with very poor success. The bigger boy was shouting as he urged on his horse: "Get along dere! I'm one of the Woodruffs and I'm boss of de road. G'long!" Nathaniel Currier came forward smiling and took the sketch from young Worth. He gave it a hasty glance and said: "This is a clever thing. We'll give you five dollars for it just as it is. You know that we will have to have it redrawn on stone to publish it."

This was the first drawing for which Worth ever received money. It was subsequently published by N. Currier, with changes, with the caption, "A Brush on the Road, Mile Heats, Best Two in Three." It was the beginning of a long line of Worth cartoons and comics, which were to prove as popular and profitable as any prints the firm produced.

Worth was never a regular employee of Currier & Ives, but he was by far the most prolific of the outside contributors. Sometime after he sold his first print to Currier he took a bundle of sketches to the offices of Harper & Brothers. There he introduced himself to Fletcher Harper, who had seen some of his work. Harper immediately took him to the head of the art department, Charles Parsons, himself an artist of some prominence who also did considerable work for Currier & Ives. Harper handed Parsons the portfolio of Worth's drawings, saying, "This is a young man whom we want to encourage all we can." Parsons too liked the drawings, and Worth was engaged. He worked for Harper & Brothers for many years.

The long series of comics that Worth did for Currier & Ives over a period of many years comprises the largest single group among the stock prints. They are divided into the Darktowns and the so-called White Comics. The Darktowns provide a humorous treatment of almost every activity of Negro life, real and imagined, from the cradle to the grave. They include burlesques of all kinds of sports—baseball (134), tennis (132), yachting (134), fox hunting (135), and the like. There are comic horse-racing pictures, scenes of watermelon- and oyster-eating contests, foot races, crap games, bicycle outings (183) and races, banjo classes, Darktown fire brigades in action, and a hundred other varied subjects. Some of them, like the fire pictures, "The Darktown Fire Brigade—Hook and Ladder Gymnastics" (133) and "The Darktown Fire Brigade—Saved!" (133), seem to burlesque the more serious Currier & Ives prints. "The Darktown Hunt—The Meet" (135), "The Darktown Hunt—Presenting the Brush" (135), "A Mule Team on an Up Grade" (25), and "A Mule Team on a Down Grade" (25) are typical.

The White Comics, though less numerous, also had great popularity. The two "Howling Swell" prints (23) and the print "A Bare Chance" (176) are representative. A series within this group was a set of railroad-train incidents, typical of which is "A 'Limited Express.' Five seconds for Refreshments!" (176).

The comics appealed to the sense of humor of many widely assorted types of people. The Duke of Newcastle, accompanying the then Prince of Wales on a tour of this country, was strolling through Nassau Street one day when he was attracted by the display in the window of the Currier & Ives store. The Darktown Comics so delighted him that he bought a full set (a hundred prints).

One Worth sketch was refused by Currier & Ives. It showed a horse reaching out of a box-stall door and removing the hat from the head of a portly and dignified gentleman. The inscription underneath it read: "Mr. Ives, of Currier & Ives Print Service, at the race track at Hartford, had his hat taken off by the celebrated black trotter 'Judge Fullerton,' one of the most vicious beasts of all time." Ives's sense of humor was good, but it is understandable that pride should have prevented his allowing this print to appear on the Currier & Ives list.

The comics by no means represented Thomas Worth's best work. The originals of the comics were wash drawings, pen-and-ink sketches, and pencil sketches. They were often very rough, and much of the real work was left to the lithographer. Much finer was his work for the trotting-horse prints. Among the best is the rare "'Trotting Cracks' at the

Forge" (79), the original Worth drawing (78) for which is reproduced here. Another lively horse print by Worth is "Fashionable 'Turn-Outs' in Central Park" (45), picturing not only smart-stepping trotters and pacers but also eight different kinds of carriages in use at that time. Worth sketched very rapidly, and this ability was especially valuable when sketches of horses and horse races had to be made on the spot. He went frequently to the tracks, often accompanied by Ives, on special assignments for the firm.

Worth was an enthusiastic sportsman himself, and his enormous fund of humor made him a pleasant, not to say riotous, companion. He was a good horseman, a crack shot, and a skillful fisherman. Evidence of Worth's intimate knowledge of fishing and salt-water sailing is shown in the print "Trolling for Blue Fish" (28), the background of which was done by Fanny Palmer, who signed the print. The catboat was drawn by Worth from memory. He liked good company and had an impressive capacity for liquor. He was, all in all, a character. The more that is found out about these old prints, the more important become the contributions of Thomas Worth.

ARTHUR FITZWILLIAM TAIT

THERE WAS PROBABLY no finer artist among those whose work was reproduced by Currier & Ives than Arthur Fitzwilliam Tait. If Louis Maurer, Thomas Worth, and the lithographer Cameron are the great triumvirate of the horse prints, Maurer, Worth, Fanny Palmer, and Tait can be said to be the rulers of the larger field of prints of sporting and outdoor life in general. Perhaps our greatest sporting artist, Tait would earn a high place in any discussion of art of the period. Among the Currier & Ives group he ranks among the very finest. He was not a Currier & Ives man in the sense that Maurer and Worth were, but among collectors the Tait prints have been the most valued and sought-after of any of the group. It is quite possible that the reproduction of his work by Currier & Ives, with which he was not always satisfied, will prove to be his chief claim to lasting fame.

The Tait prints are outstanding first of all, of course, because he was unquestionably a splendid artist of American outdoor life. In the second place his paintings were reproduced with great precision and care. Few liberties were taken with his originals. The prints made from his oil paintings were nearly always in the large folio size, selling for from one dollar and a half to three dollars. It will be remembered that these prints were sent outside the shop for coloring to men who were themselves artists. The finished product, then, represented the best work of which the shop of Currier & Ives was capable.

But the best was not always good enough to satisfy the exacting artist. His relationship with the firm differed quite sharply from that of the other artists. He was never employed by Currier & Ives, and he does not seem always to have thought willingly of his work as material for reproduction. His correspondence with the firm over a period of years reveals that he was not always satisfied either with the way his pictures were reproduced or indeed with the idea that they should be reproduced at all. In one letter to Currier, Tait objects rather strenuously to the fact that some details have been eliminated in the lithographing of his last painting. In another he complains bitterly that the sale of the lithographs has very much interfered with the sale of his paintings, going on to say that his work will largely have to be influenced by its reproduction value. Again he deplores the appearance of the name of the lithographer in as prominent a position as his own, stating very definitely that to the artist and creator belong the honors, no matter how good the lithographer's art may be. Yet in other letters he shows keen interest in the subjects that the public wants, and asks for suggestions along these lines. His attitude on the whole appears to have been contradictory, but as to the fact that he contributed largely to some of the finest Currier & Ives work there can be no argument.

Tait was of English parentage. Born near Liverpool in 1819, at fifteen he went to work with a firm of art dealers. So strong was his desire to learn about art that after a twelve-hour day at the store he would go at night to the Royal Institute in Manchester, where special arrangements were made for him to study. When he had attained a thorough knowledge of drawing he gave up his place in the store and determined to make the pursuit of art his profession. Nature and the out-of-doors had always had a fascination for him, but the restricted country of England offered few opportunities. He determined therefore to come to the United States.

He arrived in New York in 1850 and was not long in having the quality of his work recognized. Two of his first pictures were reproduced by firms other than Currier & Ives. Williams & Stevens did a steel engraving from his "Returning to Camp with Game," which includes a self-portrait of Tait in the foreground, dipping up a glass of water. His "Halt in the Woods" was reproduced by Goupil & Company.

In three years he had acquired a sufficient reputation to be made an associate of the National Academy of Design, and in 1858 he became a full academician. Tait had a studio on Broadway and a camp on Long Lake in the Adirondacks where he spent much time. Here he was visited by Maurer and other artists and sportsmen, and here he did much of his finest work. He studied nature and animal life closely, and many hours spent at hunting, fishing, and living in the wilds qualified him as an expert sportsman and woodsman.

One of his closest friends was James McDougall Hart, the landscape painter. Hart, who painted many Adirondack scenes similar to some of Tait's, is thought to have helped Tait with his backgrounds and foliage, which certainly vary widely in some of his work. It is known that their association was close, and they may well have influenced and helped each other.

The Tait pictures that were reproduced by Currier & Ives fall into several classes. The series on Indians and Western life on which Tait and Maurer collaborated include several notable ones. "A Prairie Hunter. 'One Rubbed Out,'" 1852, "Life on the Prairie. The 'Buffalo Hunt,'" 1862 (29), and "Taking the Back Track. A Dangerous Neighborhood," 1866, are among them.

"American Forest Scene. Maple Sugaring" (113), done in 1854, is noteworthy as the finest Currier & Ives print picturing this truly American custom.

In the camping folio series the outstanding ones are "Camping Out. Some of the

Right Sort," 1856, and "Camping in the Woods. A Good Time Coming," 1863. Perhaps the most interesting of the fishing prints is "Brook Trout Fishing. 'An Anxious Moment,'" 1862. This print was lithographed by Charles Parsons. Although he and Tait together made a distinguished combination, actually there are several prints that must be rated as superior. One of them is "Catching a Trout. 'We hab you now, sar!'" 1854 (15), which Otto Knirsch lithographed. It is unfortunate that these two did not work in combination oftener, for Knirsch has reproduced all the quality and movement of the Tait canvas on the stone.

Another Tait print in which Parsons appears as lithographer is "American Winter Sports. Trout Fishing 'on Chateaugay Lake,'" 1856 (124). On this folio, in the first state, appear the words "Printed by Endicott & Co." Here is evidence to indicate that Currier & Ives, in order to secure the services of Parsons, had to farm out some of their work to the company for which he worked at the time. The charming and gentle print "The Home of the Deer" (170) also is inscribed: "Painted by A. F. Tait. On Stone by C. Parsons." This print and its companion, "Sunrise on Lake Saranac" (170), along with many others by Tait are noted not only for their sporting but also for their scenic values.

In the game series the Tait prints of quail and woodcock are famous. "Snowed Up. Ruffed Grouse in Winter," 1867 (68), is one of the best of all his game pictures. "Pigeon Shooting. 'Playing the decoy'" (122) is another Tait, showing an old American sport that is nearly forgotten today. Among the shooting pictures the series "American Field Sports," all done in 1857, are unquestionably the finest. The four prints have the subtitles "A Chance for Both Barrels," "Flush'd" (17), "On a Point," and "Retrieving." The original Tait oil painting for "Flush'd" (16) is also reproduced here. Comparison between it and the print will reveal how faithfully the lithographer worked.

The record price ever paid for a Currier & Ives print was recorded in 1928 at the sale of the Norman James Collection for Tait's "The Life of a Hunter. 'A tight fix'" (10). This picture, showing a hunter wielding a bloody knife against a wounded and enraged grizzly bear while another hunter tries to draw a bead on the bear's head, was sold for the unprecedented price of $3,000. The companion print "Catching a Tartar" has not caught the popular fancy to the same extent. "Mink Trapping. 'Prime,'" 1862 (50), is another that is very rare, while one entitled "In the Mountains," a large folio print of deer, undated, has never yet been found. This latter title appears in the copyright records in Washington, and without doubt the print to match it will someday come to light.

Tait also did a number of dead-game panels. These have been in great demand in recent years and seldom appear at auction. There are many others that deserve mention, but not so many as to satisfy the demand of today's market. A collection of the Tait prints alone would form a magnificent gallery, representative of the best of the Currier & Ives list.

FANNY PALMER

THERE IS NO MORE interesting and appealing character among the group of artists who worked for Currier & Ives than Fanny Palmer. In an age when women, well-bred women in particular, did not generally work for a living Fanny Palmer for years did exacting, full-time work in order to support a large and dependent family. It is impossible to establish accurately the number of Currier & Ives prints to which Fanny Palmer contributed, but it was enormous. No single artist, not even Worth or Maurer, contributed so much in so many varied ways.

Fanny Palmer, born Frances Flora Bond, came to New York from England in the early forties with her husband, Edward S. Palmer. With them also came their two children and Mrs. Palmer's sister and brother, Maria and Robert Bond. They all came from Leicester and were, by birth, training, and background, gentlefolk. Mrs. Palmer and her sister had attended a very select private school in London and there had been well instructed in music, the fine arts, and literature. It seems probable that they grew up in some luxury, but at the time when they came to America they were very poor. Apparently they hoped to find a better outlet for their talents and to effect a change in their circumstances in the new country.

The two sisters were charming, cultivated, talented, and brave and by no means too proud to earn their own living. Robert Bond, too, although his talents were a trifle precious for the America of the forties, was energetic and able. A graduate of Eton, he was an accomplished singer, played the pianoforte well, and was adept at drawing and painting. He established an office and studio on Fulton Street and achieved no little fame painting very popular still-lifes of fruit and flowers. He also made architectural drawings and gave lessons in singing and pianoforte.

Edward Palmer pursued no other trade than that of being a "gentleman." He was fond of shooting, even fonder of drinking, and had no interest in any kind of work. As time went on his son became a handsome second edition of his father.

Since Robert's earnings alone could not support the family, both Fanny Palmer and her sister went to work. The family had settled in Brooklyn, and from among their wealthy and socially prominent friends the two sisters, and later Mrs. Palmer's daughter, found pupils in singing, painting, and the making of wax flowers, then in great vogue. They also acted as governesses and as chaperons to young girls on excursions. Maria Bond also taught music, painting, and drawing in the Misses Day's private school for many years.

But Fanny Palmer was really the breadwinner. Just when she first went to work for Currier & Ives is not known, but Louis Maurer remembered that when he joined the staff in 1852 Mrs. Palmer had already been with them for some time. She was a small, frail woman with large, dark eyes and a typically English complexion, on the whole rather plain in appearance but possessing a delightful personality. She worked for Currier & Ives, either as a regular employee or on piecework, until her death in 1876 at the age of sixty-four. In later years her back became so stooped from long hours of overwork that she appeared almost deformed.

Almost from the beginning Mrs. Palmer specialized in securing atmosphere and background. She would be driven in Currier's carriage out into Long Island, where she would sketch rapidly all types of rural and suburban scenery. She often sketched on both sides of the paper, using a very soft pencil. Often there would be two different treatments of the same scene, features from both of which would be used in the finished print. Country scenes, lanes and cottages, toll gates, mills and farmhouses are among the most familiar of her works. Sometimes figures were added by Maurer, Knirsch, or Venino.

It will be remembered that Fanny Palmer frequently colored the models that were followed by the colorists, and that she also worked with Charles Currier in the development and manufacture of his famous lithographic crayons. There seems to have been no task to which she was unwilling to set her hand. For much of her work she received no credit on the finished print. As we have seen, the lithographers often appended only their own names, ignoring that of the artist altogether. Then too, unlike Thomas Worth, who signed his drawings in a bold and sprawling hand and in a place where the lithographer could hardly miss it, Fanny Palmer, when she signed her sketches at all, did so inconspicuously. But any study and comparison of the prints will reveal that Mrs. Palmer unquestionably had a hand in very many of the unsigned ones, as well as in the substantial number that bear her name.

It is probable, too, that the other members of her family, Maria, Robert, and perhaps even her daughter, worked on sketches with her. There are buildings in some of her prints that do not look like her work, and these and some of the unsigned fruit and flower prints might well have been the work of Robert Bond. So great is the mass of prints with which the name of Fanny Palmer must inevitably be connected that the theory that some of them must have been a family or group effort seems the most logical.

Representative samples of the varied work by Mrs. Palmer that are reproduced here include the stirring railroad prints "The 'Lightning Express' Trains" (19) and "American Express Train" (70), also her picturesque and vivid Mississippi series, "The Mississippi in Time of Peace" (112), "The Mississippi in Time of War" (100), "'High Water' in the Mississippi" (34), "Low Water in the Mississippi" (56), and "'Wooding Up' on the Mississippi" (139). Fanny Palmer proved her versatility in her excellent hunting and wild-life scenes with such examples as "Woodcock Shooting" (69) and "Partridge Shooting" (108), in which her models were her husband and his dogs, "The Happy Family. Ruffed Grouse and Young" (109), and "The Trout Stream" (51). The print "The Happy Family. Ruffed Grouse and Young" is a typical example of the fine large folios. It is one of a set of three, of which the other two are "The Cares of a Family" of quail and "A Rising Family" of snipe, both by Arthur Tait. Here should be noted the excellent unsigned print "Beach Snipe Shooting" (142), which is so typical of early American shore-bird shooting that, aside from its high pictorial quality, it takes a place in the first rank. Other interesting unsigned sporting and wild-life prints for which Fanny Palmer may well have been responsible are "The Trout Pool" (171), "Black Bass Spearing" (171), "Bear Hunting" (75), "Woodcock Shooting" (75), "Wood-Ducks" (75), "Shooting on the Prairie" (75), "English Snipe" (18), and "Prairie Hens" (18).

Mrs. Palmer was also the artist of such fine scenic prints as "Mount Washington and the White Mountains" (71) and "View of San Francisco, California" (119), the distinctive still-life print "Landscape, Fruit and Flowers" (39), and the marine prints "Clipper Ship 'Hurricane'" (126) and "Royal Mail Steam Ship 'Asia'" (147). These are only a few examples of her output, and it must be remembered that in addition this energetic woman did a great amount of background and color work for prints by other artists.

In 1859 Edward Palmer surprised no one by falling downstairs while intoxicated and breaking his neck. James Ives, on hearing this, is said to have remarked, "That's the best thing he ever did." Palmer died soon thereafter, and three years later his son, who had been little comfort to his mother, died of tuberculosis at the age of thirty-three.

Fanny Palmer's life can hardly have been a happy one, but she left behind her a not inconsiderable monument, not only in the distinction of her prolific work but also in the genuine respect and affection that her associates felt for her.

The many prints made from her drawings record an astonishing proportion of the American scene. Her work, while perhaps not the equal of that of some of the more distinguished Currier & Ives artists, had great charm, homeliness, and a conscientious attention to detail. Her major contribution was to the backbone of the Currier & Ives list, the great mass of cheap prints that sold at ridiculously low prices to the great mass of the people, a simple, uncritical, but hugely appreciative audience.

GEORGE HENRY DURRIE

A FAVORITE Currier & Ives artist for many collectors is George Henry Durrie. Currier & Ives reproduced comparatively few of his paintings, only a dozen or so in all, but his work has such authentic charm and rural flavor and such truly American character that the few prints which were produced are among the most valued of any in the entire gallery. Durrie was "the New England farm-scene painter" and was sometimes, because of his predilection for winter scenes, known as the "snowman" of the group. Several of his paintings are now in the collections of the New York Public Library and Yale University.

Born in 1820 in New Haven, Connecticut, Durrie lived there nearly all his life. He was of staunch Puritan stock and was himself a devoutly religious man. He had a fine tenor voice and for many years sang in a church choir in New Haven. He would never enter his studio on Sunday for fear that he might be tempted to pick up a brush and start work. His frank and gentle disposition was reflected in his work. He liked to paint scenes of quiet and peaceful beauty, but his paintings did not lack character or realism.

He opened his New Haven studio when he was twenty-one. At first he painted portraits, but quickly turned to his real work, New England farm-life painting. His observation was keen. He looked carefully at what he was painting, and the minuteness and accuracy of his detail are remarkable. His studies of rocks, barks, lichens, and mosses reveal his interest in the minutiae of nature. His paintings as a group form one of our best records of the old days on the New England farm, a record of a way of life that is fast vanishing.

Among the prints "The Old Homestead in Winter" is typical. "Autumn in New England. Cider Making" is valuable social history, just as is Tait's "American Forest Scene. Maple Sugaring" (113). Equally interesting and even finer from an artistic point of view is the lovely "Winter in the Country. Getting Ice" (30). This print is now very rare and high in price, although twenty years ago copies could be bought for ten or twenty dollars. "Winter in the Country. The Old Grist Mill," "Winter in the Country. A Cold Morning," and "Winter Morning. Feeding the Chickens" all have the same rural beauty and homeliness. Durrie's "Home to Thanksgiving" (2), which is a handsome piece of work, typically American, is perhaps the most widely known Currier & Ives print in this country today. It is to be regretted that his original painting for this print has never been found.

CHARLES PARSONS

ALONG WITH the trotting-horse prints of Worth and Maurer and the sporting pictures of Arthur Fitzwilliam Tait, the large group of marine prints by various artists must have equal rank as among the finest that the firm of Currier & Ives produced. The marines include roughly three hundred prints of clipper ships, river and sound steamboats, whalers, steamships, cutters, yachts, schooners, frigates, ships of the line, and naval scenes of the War of 1812 and of the Mexican War and Civil War. Among the marine artists the outstanding name is that of Charles Parsons.

Even leaving his work on the marines out of consideration, Parsons would deserve special mention as a Currier & Ives artist. We have already seen that in order to secure his services as lithographer for some of the Tait oil paintings Currier & Ives were willing to farm out work to Endicott & Company, for whom he worked. He was the artist also of the famous "Central-Park, Winter. The Skating Pond" (3), as colorful, detailed, and altogether delightful as any print on the Currier & Ives list. He too was largely responsible for most of the really good locomotive prints, including the startling "An American Railway Scene, at Hornellsville, Erie Railway" (65), which it will be readily guessed was used by the Erie as an advertisement. The scenic print "The Rail Road Suspension Bridge. Near Niagara Falls" (14) was also his work, as well as many others that are memorable. But it is among the marine artists that he stands out as a giant.

Like Tait and Fanny Palmer, Charles Parsons was of English parentage. He was born in Rowland's Castle, Havent, England in 1821, and came to America with his parents when he was nine years of age. When he was twelve he was apprenticed to George Endicott, of the firm of Endicott & Company, and went to live at his employer's home. After two years he told Endicott that he did not want to work any longer as a "boy," and a place was found for him in the company's lithographing department. Until he was twenty-one he went to night school regularly, spending what spare time he had reading and studying. Gradually he was given control of Endicott & Company's art department. Currier & Ives gave out a good deal of work to Parsons' firm during this time, and on many of the plates Parsons himself did the lithography.

In 1863 Parsons joined Harper & Brothers as head of their art department, and continued in this capacity until his retirement in 1892. Throughout the years he maintained a close friendship with both Currier and Ives and their families. He did many originals for the firm, particularly marines, which were his first love and the field of his greatest triumphs. "The Great Ocean Yacht Race. Between the 'Henrietta,' 'Fleetwing' & 'Vesta'" (76) and "Clipper Ship 'Comet' of New York" (117) are two prints representing two classes of marine subjects. Other prints produced by Parsons presented here are "Clipper Ship 'Nightingale'" (89), done by Parsons himself, and "Summer Scenes in New York Harbor" (141) and "The New York Yacht Club Regatta" (111), by Parsons and Atwater.

Currier & Ives went to Parsons constantly for help and advice. He was very sympathetic toward the struggles of young and little-known artists and frequently recommended men for special jobs.

James E. Butterworth, an Englishman by birth, was a marine artist of note, and many of his fine clipper-ship paintings were reproduced by Currier & Ives, with Charles Parsons frequently doing the lithographing. Three of Butterworth's outstanding prints reproduced here are "Clipper Ship 'Flying Cloud'" (137), "Clipper Ship 'Great Republic'" (129), and the forceful "The Wreck of the Steam Ship 'San Francisco'" (20). Another name appearing frequently in the marine prints is that of J. B. Smith & Son, Brooklyn, L. I. Several splendid prints are credited to this firm, about which unfortunately little is known. The print "Clipper Ship 'Red Jacket'" (106), by J. B. Smith & Son, is especially attractive.

To complete the collection the following marine prints by lesser artists of the time and by artists whose names are not now known are included: "Clipper Ship 'Dreadnought' off Tuskar Light" (110), by D. McFarlane; "The Celebrated Yacht 'America'" (138); the vivid whaling prints "The Whale Fishery. The Sperm Whale 'in a Flurry'" (60) and "American Whalers Crushed in the Ice" (190); "Pilot Boat 'Wm. J. Romer'" (146); and the shipwreck prints "The Steam Ship 'President'" (151) and "Loss of the Steamboat 'Swallow'" (151). Further marine prints include "The Iron Steam Ship 'Great Britain'" (182), "The Mammoth Iron Steam-Ship 'Great Eastern' 22,500 Tons, 3000 Horse Power" (35), and "The Chinese Junk 'Keying'" (182). Also reproduced are the marine naval prints "Perry's Victory on Lake Erie" (166), "M'Donough's Victy. on Lake Champlain" (166), and the panoramic Civil War print "The Splendid Naval Triumph on the Mississippi, April 24th, 1862" (140).

In the marine prints, just as in the pictures of other phases of national life at that time, Currier & Ives gave the American people what they wanted and succeeded in handing down to us true and vivid pictures of those great ships and the hardy men who sailed them.

A rather unusual print that can be included under marine subjects is "Plan of Gilbert's Balance Floating Dry Dock" (130). The print was made to support the claims of superiority of Gilbert's dry dock over the claims of other dry-dock manufacturers who had had similar prints published. The plan is interesting as a lithograph, and undoubtedly there were many other such prints made that have not yet appeared or that have not been identified as the work of Currier & Ives.

V. THE PRINTS

AT THIS POINT it is necessary to repeat that during the life of the continuing firm of Currier & Ives the number of pictures reproduced was between seven and eight thousand. It is definitely known that there are well over seven thousand different prints, and nearly every month brings to light a new or hitherto unknown one. It must be stated that, owing to the discerning taste of the American public, most of the important prints have been saved and that considerable time has passed since an important rediscovery of a print has been made that has not already been listed and catalogued by collectors. From the standpoint of modern collectors it is to be regretted that this old firm did not leave a complete and detailed list of its achievements.

Views. The prints that have been used to illustrate this volume have been chosen primarily because they are typically American both in their sources and treatment. One exception is the print "The Lakes of Killarney" (136), which is a graphic view, full of detail, and one of the best views issued by Currier & Ives. That the firm did a number of Irish prints can be accounted for by the large migration to this country from Ireland during the second half of the nineteenth century and by the desire of the immigrants to have pictures of their homeland.

Little is known about the artists who were responsible for the long and important series of views. The names of the artists that have come down to us as doing a large part of the work are Fanny Palmer, Voltaire Combe, and J. Schultz. These particular artists produced most of the prints of scenes in and around New York City. New York, then as now, was not only the home of Currier & Ives but was also the focal point for European immigration during that period. Then too the Hudson River was the gateway to the new territories by way of the Erie Canal, which had been completed in 1825. Included among the New York views are "Upper and Lower Bay of New York" (150), "The Entrance to the Highlands" (131), and the two pleasing prints called "View of New York" (172). Perhaps the most favored of these prints is Charles Parsons' "Central-Park, Winter" (3). The detail of costume in this print has been used frequently in the clothing of actors for modern stage and motion-picture productions. The print "The Old Stone House. L.I., 1699" (64) was drawn in the countryside on Long Island, where Fanny Palmer and other Currier & Ives artists used to roam, seeking material and inspiration for their sketches.

Three important prints in the views series that have been included here are "View of Harpers Ferry, Va." (179), "The Falls of Niagara" (114), and the scarce and early print, "Dartmouth College" (125). Two delightful prints are those of Washington Irving's home "Sunny Side" (168) and "The Mill-Dam at 'Sleepy Hollow'" (168), the latter spot made famous by Irving's great story *The Legend of Sleepy Hollow*. The print "Newport Beach" (150) is also an important view because it pictures a location on the Atlantic seacoast that was to become famous in later years, also because the print was drawn in a manner that foreshadowed the modern techniques of painting seascapes.

During the middle years of the firm two prints were produced that for detail, general interest, and national importance are outstanding contributions. These prints have been reproduced in the present volume: "Burning of the New York Crystal Palace" (120) and "Great Conflagration at Pittsburgh Pa." (72). At about the same period the great movement into the West, which reached its peak in the Gold Rush of '49, opened a new field and supplied a fresh impetus not only to Currier & Ives but to other lithographers as well. One of the finest prints produced later to commemorate this transcontinental advance was done by Currier & Ives: "The Rocky Mountains. Emigrants Crossing the Plains" (40). This print is also known as the Covered Wagon print and is a memorial to those hardy pioneers who crossed the continent from the Atlantic to the Pacific in oxen-drawn prairie schooners. The Covered Wagon print is the work of Fanny Palmer. In this category can also be included "The Way They Come from California" (186), an important print from a set of six cartoons drawn in New York by an unknown artist. It must be admitted that the artist of this print depended more on imagination than on actual fact.

Political Cartoons and Banners. Another group of prints that can be mentioned briefly are the political cartoons and banners, which provide us with an insight into the stormy political era of the last century and which in their way are unique creations. While not comparable to the masterly drawings of Daumier, Rowlandson, Gillray, and Tenniel, these broadsheet lithographic cartoons do have a sincerity and wholesomeness, a simplicity of composition and a Daguerrean sureness of detail. The cartoon artists included such notable figures as Thomas Nast, Louis Maurer, Ben Day, and J. Cameron. The conversational balloon was used, the figures were immobile and photographic, and there was little about the prints that resembled a caricature. The main idea appears to have been to inform the people of political crises and to make that report visually. When political feeling was running high the firm deleted its name from the cartoons, sometimes simply adding the line, "For sale at 2 Spruce Street." This precaution seems hardly necessary in view of the conservative nature of the cartoons.

The most popular of these cartoons were "A Philosopher in Ecstasy" (153), "A Serviceable Garment" (153), "The Great Republican Reform Party" (155), "Progressive Democracy—Prospect of a Smash Up" (157), "Running the 'Machine'" (161), and "The Rail Candidate" (162). The two prints "The Modern Colossus. Eighth Wonder of the World" (154) and "The Presidential Fishing Party of 1848" (154) were copyrighted in 1848 by a Peter Smith, 2 Spruce Street, N. Y. Since none of the early directories lists Peter Smith, and as No. 2 Spruce Street was occupied by N. Currier in 1848, it is safe to assume that Currier thought it best to publish his first political cartoons under a pseudonym. In support of this interpretation is the fact that many Peter Smith cartoons were sold in the final remainder sale of Currier & Ives. One of the most characteristic of the pro-Lincoln political cartoons is "Honest Abe Taking Them on the Half Shell" (121), drawn by Louis Maurer and typical of the artist's best work in this particular field.

An important print that cannot be omitted is "The Age of Brass" (164). It was the first lithographic print of those political activities of women of the last century that were later to become the Suffrage movement. The print "Grand Democratic Free Soil Banner" (105), carrying the portraits of Martin Van Buren and Charles F. Adams, is a fine example of the campaign banners issued by Currier & Ives. Considerable importance was attached to these banners by the firm, the Free Soil banner going a long way toward making Van Buren one of the most publicized men of his time. Currier & Ives invented and promoted this type of campaign banner, and during active political periods it was one of the largest-selling items produced by the firm.

Portraits. One of the largest contributions of the firms of N. Currier and Currier & Ives was the group of nearly five hundred portraits, which comprised a pictorial who's who of mid-nineteenth-century America. This group also included a number of portraits of foreign celebrities that were turned out for consumption by those people who had recently migrated to America. The portrait that was the first to bear the Currier imprint, that of Dr. Dewees of the University of Pennsylvania, printed in 1834, is one of the finest lithographic portraits produced in America. Since this portrait was not done in the universal style, Currier & Ives later adjusted themselves to issue portraits as stock-size prints. One of the best of the later portraits was that of "Sara Bernhardt" (149), which was issued during the last years of the old firm. The Dewees portrait and the portrait of Benjamin Franklin are prints most eagerly sought by the modern collector.

Presidents and important American statesmen were not neglected. The portraits of the early group of the presidential series from Washington to Lincoln are of a higher quality than the later and more hurriedly sketched portraits. This may be accounted for in part by the fact that the portraits of the first five presidents were reproduced by Currier & Ives artists from the famous Gilbert Stuart paintings. Prints of the presidential series that are reproduced here are the portraits "George Washington. First President of the United States" (159), "Hon. Abraham Lincoln. Republican Candidate for Sixteenth President of the United States" (160), "James Madison. Fourth President of the United

States" (104), "Thomas Jefferson. Third President of the United States" (104), "Martin Van Buren. Eighth President of the United States" (104), and "William Henry Harrison. Ninth President of the United States" (104). One of the more elaborate portraits shown is "Washington's Reception by the Ladies, on Passing the Bridge at Trenton, N.J. April 1789" (105).

Historical Prints. Another large and important group is that of the historical prints, many of which were copied from well-known paintings of that time. Perhaps the most outstanding of these prints are three that were copies from the original paintings of John Trumbull: "The Declaration of Independence" (180), "Surrender of Cornwallis" (177), and "Surrender of General Burgoyne at Saratoga N.Y. Oct. 17th 1777" (99). The original oil paintings now hang in Yale University. Some of the more important historical prints that were chosen to illustrate this volume are "Marion's Brigade Crossing the Pedee River, S.C. 1778" (47), "General Francis Marion, of South Carolina. In his swamp Encampment; inviting a British Officer to share his Dinner of sweet Potatoes and cold Water" (185), "Cornwallis Is Taken!" (37), and "Capture of Andre 1780" (37). All of these prints have a picturesque quality that is truly American. This gallery of historic scenes could never have been considered complete by Nathaniel Currier had it not included "The Birth-Place of Washington" (73) and the delightful print that is so often seen today, "Washington's Dream" (152). The last episode of George Washington's military career has been commemorated by Currier & Ives in "Washington Taking Leave of the Officers of His Army" (185).

A beginner in the collecting of Currier & Ives prints desiring to enter into a wide and virtually untouched field might well choose the Civil War historical prints. Since there is a certain sameness to a number of the Civil War prints, collectors have neglected them to a degree, but there are some in the group that do have great historical value, as is shown in "Bombardment of Fort Sumter, Charleston Harbor" (37) and in "The Fall of Richmond Va. on the Night of April 2nd 1865" (37). The print "The Battle of Fair Oaks, Va. May 31st 1862" (128) is an exceptionally fine example of the alert news sense of Currier & Ives and their use of historical timeliness, since in this picture is seen a representation of the first captive balloon ever used for warfare observation. An interesting sidelight on this print is that one of the persons in the captive balloon was the young Count Zeppelin, who later developed the lighter-than-air craft that was to bear his name.

There is also a group of prints, difficult to classify, that deal with the grimmer side of life during Civil War days. Examples of these are "John Brown—the Martyr" (118) and "The Body of the Martyr President, Abraham Lincoln" (118). It is known from contemporary records that the latter print had a tremendous sale and appeared in two or three different lithographic states. Another print that can be included in this category is "The Story of the Fight" (181), which depicts a wounded soldier, who has returned home, telling the story of the battle. Two outstanding historical prints are "Landing of the Pilgrims at Plymouth 11th Dec. 1620" (180) and "Franklin's Experiment, June 1752" (26). The historical prints indicate the keen sense of news values possessed by Currier & Ives, which was skillfully applied to coincide with public tastes of the day.

Certificates, Moral and Religious Prints. At this time a curious type of sentimentality in the national life found expression in the production of a great number of printed certificates that were filled in with ink at the time of a birth, entry into a church, a marriage, or a death. Two types of these prints that are reproduced here are "Marriage Certificate" (12) and, in the case of a death, "In Memory Of" (66). This phase of Americana that called the sentimental prints into being was of considerable importance, and special note must be made of such a work as "The Art of Making Money Plenty in Every Man's Pocket, by Doctor Franklin" (27), which is actually a clever and early rebus. "The Tree of Life. The Christian" (86), "The Drunkards Progress. From the First Glass to the Grave" (90), and "The Bad Man at the Hour of Death" (123) are definite expressions of a large and popular group of moral, religious, and didactic pictures that were extremely popular. From the great number of sentimental prints produced it is certain that they had a wide and active sale throughout the long existence of Currier & Ives.

Religion was an exceptionally potent factor in those days, so it is safe to assume that a large number of the Currier & Ives religious prints were made to order. Most of these prints were copies of famous European paintings and had a sizable sale both in this country and abroad. One of the prints that is a striking exception shows a typically American scene: "Shakers near Lebanon" (26), picturing a Shaker meeting in progress in a New York meetinghouse.

Sentimental Prints. How to account for the tastes that were instrumental in producing Lord Byron's "Mazeppa" (44), a series of four prints each with verses of the poem attached, is rather difficult at this time. They belong in the extravagant category that included "My Child! My Child!" (165) and "They're Saved! They're Saved!" (165). The only possible explanation is that Currier & Ives advertised that they had prints for all tastes.

The sentimental portraits and sentimental scenes comprise a delightful and amusing group that is outstanding for its wide variety of subject matter and often distinguished by exceptionally fine workmanship. "The Bloomer Costume" (95), "The Flower Girl" (42), "Isabella" (48), "Julia" (42), "Emeline" (48), "The Sisters" (102), and "Highland Fling" (46) are typical of a group for which Fanny Palmer and perhaps the lithographer Venino were largely responsible. "The Lovers Walk" (148), "The Morning Recreation" (148), "Black Eyed Susan" (148), "My First Love" (83), "The Lovers Quarrel" (11) and "The Lovers Reconciliation" (11), "The Sailors Adieu" (6) and "The Sailor's Return" (6), the similar pair dedicated to the soldier (7), "Popping the Question" (8), "Single" (13), "Married" (13), and "The Marriage" (98) are only a few of the scores of prints dealing sentimentally and fondly with partings, returns, love, and marriage. The print "Black Eyed Susan" attracted the attention of Charles Dickens and caused him to write that the American public was exceedingly picture-minded and that these gaily colored pictures appeared in many places. He was particularly impressed by the fact that when Queen Victoria appeared in a print and was hung on the walls in America she was presented as a very young and beautiful person. In the undated N. Currier print "Queen Victoria" (96) this observation is seen to have been quite true. From such prints as "An Increase of

Family" (192) and "The Trial of Patience" (192) can be gained a mass of information regarding dress, house furnishings, and family customs from that period in which Currier & Ives flourished. Similar prints, differing only in their out-of-doors setting, are "Holidays in the Country" (191), "The Old Barn Floor" (191), and "Harvest" (33). In these prints, just as in the delightful "The Star of the Road" (38), which is the representation of a well-dressed young woman, are shown more details of the costumes of that day.

Prints for Children. Children of the last century were not forgotten in the vast gallery of Currier & Ives. "Robinson Crusoe and His Pets" (82) and "Noah's Ark" (82) are two children's prints that appear to have been great favorites. The author of this volume has an amusing letter in his collection that was addressed to the firm of Currier & Ives in which the woman writing the letter stated that she wanted the original print of "Noah's Ark," the one that showed the snake. It seems that she had previously received the third lithographic state of the print and this detail had been omitted. Another group of prints, known as puzzle pictures, in which one could search for hidden figures drawn into the background of the picture, was probably also created for children. There are only six of these prints known, and the best of the group is "The Puzzled Fox" (54).

Country and Pioneer Home Scenes. A number of prints were issued by Currier & Ives that dealt with country and pioneer home scenes, as for example "The Western Farmers Home" (53), which is of the frontier type, "The Thatched Cottage" (53), "Frozen Up" (53), "American Forest Scene" (113), and "Maple Sugaring" (53). In the lovely print "Early Winter" (115) and in the somewhat primitive one "A Clearing" (63) can again be seen the efforts of Currier & Ives to serve the tastes of all their customers and to show every phase of American life. "A Suburban Retreat" (63) and "Hudson River—Crow Nest" (63) were produced to be sold close to New York City. With these should be listed "Gems of American Scenery" (74), one of the few prints in which more than one scene is pictured. It must be stated that this procedure of grouping four pictures together was unusual for Currier & Ives. The making of prints in series or blocks of four, six, eight, and even more pictures was customary with European lithographers, but it was seldom done by printmakers in this country.

Humor. It is a fact that little humor was introduced into the early Currier & Ives prints, and it is now believed that the artists were too preoccupied to produce much of this kind of work. An exception is the amusing print "Kiss Me Quick" (97), which is perhaps crude, but which is outstanding among prints of its kind.

Lithographed Sheet Music. During this period it was the practice of lithographers to print pictures that would dress up the appearance of sheet music and make the music scores more salable. Many lithographers who were contemporaries of Currier & Ives graduated from general lithography to become sheet-music publishers exclusively. Throughout the life of the firm Currier & Ives produced a large number of these music sheets with lithographic illustrations. The earliest work of this kind was perhaps done by Nathaniel Currier himself when he was a lithographer working for Pendleton and which he carried on during the partnership of Currier & Stodart. There are four known music sheets issued by Currier & Stodart dated 1834 that have survived to this day. More interesting sheet-music prints done later by Currier & Ives are "La Mazurka danced in 'La Gitana' by Madame Taglioni" (91), "The New York Light Guard's Quick Step" (92), "Our Boat Sets Lightly on the Wave" (93), and "Charter Oak" (94). Although this group shows fine workmanship, the firm of Currier & Ives made no great effort to occupy a large place in the field of sheet-music lithography.

Mississippi River Prints. One of the more important and handsome group of prints produced by the firm is that which has to do with the Mississippi River. Pictures of those early epic days on the Mississippi, with the attendant romance and drama of the passenger packet and showboat, are everywhere lacking except as they are found in the Currier & Ives gallery. In addition to the Fanny Palmer Mississippi scenes that have previously been referred to, the prints "On the Mississippi. Loading Cotton" (87) and "Bound Down the River" (87) show a wealth of detail in their composition and bring back to us the romantic flavor of Mississippi River scenes of the last century. The two picturesque prints "Midnight Race on the Mississippi" (101) and "Through the Bayou by Torchlight" (101) were especially outstanding as great lithographic accomplishments of their day. Often some of the standard Mississippi prints were re-used as advertisements for the traveling *Uncle Tom's Cabin* companies, known at that time as Tom Shows. An example of a Tom Show print is "Steamboat Race on the Mississippi. Act IV, Scene III. Jarrett & Palmer's Revival of Uncle Tom's Cabin" (43), which was also issued, with the advertising omitted, as a standard print.

Railroad Prints. Later the railroad, which made its appearance in America during the lifetime of Nathaniel Currier and James Ives, to some degree supplanted the boats that plied the Mississippi and Hudson rivers and gave the firm the opportunity to supply its customers with the best early transportation prints that were available. The prints "The 'Lightning Express' Trains. 'Leaving the Junction'" (19) and the two "Express Train" prints (188), because of the accuracy and minuteness of their technical drawing, are very real documents as well as delightful lithographs. Many of these pictures, such as "The Danger Signal" (32) and "An American Railway Scene, at Hornellsville, Erie Railway" (65), were used as advertisements for the railroads—some of them after they had been issued as stock prints.

This tendency toward the using of lithographic prints as advertising media can possibly be attributed to the close personal friendship of Nathaniel Currier and P. T. Barnum. Not only were the two men closely associated during this period, but a number of Currier & Ives prints pictured oddities that were to be seen in Barnum's Museum. In all probability these were the work of the artist Sarony, since a number of similar prints were signed by him. "The Man that Gave Barnum His 'Turn'" (77) is a good-natured ribbing given the great showman by the partners, showing "Before" and "After" portraits of an unkempt Irishman who gave his turn in the barbershop to Barnum. The latter offered to pay the Irishman's bill if he would let Barnum precede him. Barnum went first, whereupon the Celt ordered everything the barbershop had to offer. The print, which tells the whole story, has an insert in which the barber is shown presenting the man's bill of $1.60 to the astonished Barnum.

Emancipation, Speculation. In studying this large group of prints it is surprising to discover that the subject of emancipation, which was receiving universal attention at that time, was almost completely neglected by the firm. This fact can probably be attributed to the controversial nature of the subject. One of the rarer prints on this topic is "Branding Slaves, on the Coast of Africa Previous to Embarkation" (81). Generally speaking, Currier & Ives avoided this particular subject with scrupulous care, yet they approached another matter, that of financial speculation in its broader sense, which was receiving a great deal of condemnation in the newspapers of their day. They produced a series of prints, examples of which are "Stocks Up" and "Stocks Down" (174), that indicate that this tendency to speculate was already very much a part of the American scene at that early period in our history.

Horse Prints. Lithographic prints having horses as their chief subject were one of the principal outputs of Currier & Ives, who were the acknowledged specialists in their time of the horse print proper. A study of the other four hundred odd lithographers of that day discloses that all of them combined did not produce as many prints on this subject as did Currier & Ives alone. It is also a fact that the firm spared neither time nor expense in assembling the finest horse-artist staff of that period. On looking back to those days it is difficult for us to realize the prime significance of the horse to our forefathers, yet it is true that this astute firm issued over six hundred prints testifying to the importance of the horse in that period in the history of America. It can be truly said that there has never been made a similar record of the growth and development of any phase of agriculture or the breeding of animals that can compare with the horse-print gallery of Currier & Ives. The great sales impetus of these prints was perhaps aided by the American desire, then as now, for displays of speed. At any rate the country was so vitally interested in the popular phrase of that day, "knocking the seconds down," that whenever an American trotter clipped a second or two off an established record it was news of national importance. At this time, before the days of wide national advertising, the trotting horse was also the magnet that drew large crowds to the country fairs and did its part in attracting attention to products displayed at the fairs.

The print "Mac and Zachary Taylor in the Great Contest at Hunting Park Course Phila. July 18th 1849" (59), which is quaintly subtitled "For the Championship of the Turf. Mac, Victorious," is especially interesting because it pictures trotting horses being raced under saddle. This was necessary at that time because country roads had not yet been developed to the point where one could go very far in a horse-drawn vehicle. Another important print is "Dutchman" (62), which is a picture of the first horse to trot twenty miles within an hour. This feat had been attempted a number of times before, but Dutchman was the first horse to finish this race against time and still survive the effort. Both of these prints were reproduced from paintings by famous artists of the period. Henri Delattre, a Frenchman who came to this country in the suite of Louis Napoleon, produced the original painting of "Mac and Zachary Taylor" (58), while the original "Dutchman" painting was the work of Edward Troye, who migrated to America from Switzerland, later to become one of the greatest horse painters the world has ever known. Another print reproduced from a contemporary painting is "Lady Suffolk and Lady Moscow" (173). Lady Suffolk, shown in the foreground in the print, was also known as "The Old Grey Mare of Long Island." After traveling through seventeen states on her own feet, she established a world's record in her nineteenth year.

One of the outstanding racing prints, which is also an excellent sporting scene, is "Peytona & Fashion. In Their Great Match for $20,000" (9). This is of course a print, not of trotting, but of running racing, and is unusual because it is the first large sporting print of this type produced in America. The match also aroused added interest because it was heralded as a race between the North and the South. Peytona, owned by Thomas Kirkman of Alabama, won the match beating Fashion, owned by Henry K. Toler, in the best two out of three four-mile heats.

The print "George M. Patchen, Brown Dick and Millers Damsel" (173) is interesting because Miller's Damsel turned out to be a great fountainhead of the blood lines of the modern American race horse. At the time of Currier & Ives horses were just horses, and if they trotted better they were driven, or if they rode better they were ridden. It was Miller's Damsel who, when bred to different sires, produced colts that were specialized as racing thoroughbreds or American trotters. That same specialization has continued to this day.

An unusual horse print that is somewhat out of the standard horse-print category is "A Correct Likeness of Mr. H. Rockwell's Horse Alexander, Bowery Amphitheatre, New York March 17th 1840" (52). This is purely an advertising print, the order for it having been given by the Bowery Amphitheatre, one of the earliest American circuses, to Currier & Ives because of the firm's outstanding staff of horse artists and because of its success in producing fine horse prints. This particular print is an example of the kind of work that the firm was also accustomed to do for P. T. Barnum.

Sporting Events. Sporting events as presented in the Currier & Ives gallery are somewhat difficult to classify. In those days little time was devoted to sport as a source of entertainment for spectators. Crowds did attend the trotting and running races, but behind their interest in these contests as sporting events was their interest in the horses themselves, horses being the principal means of transportation for rich and poor alike.

Although the figures are slightly stilted in the prize-fighting print "The Great Fight for the Championship" (55), it does give an interesting picture of a prize-fight scene as it was attended by Currier & Ives contemporaries. The firm also issued a host of portraits picturing outstanding pugilists of the day. Examples of these portraits that are reproduced here are "Tom Sayers Champion of England" (145) and "John Morrissey" (145).

Sailing races as pictured in the Currier & Ives marine prints were, of course, sporting events, and besides the prints of sailing races a large number of boating prints such as "The Great International Boat Race Aug. 27th 1869" (178) were issued. Another important sport of those early days that has continued its existence up to the present time is iceboating, as shown in the print "Ice-Boat Race on the Hudson" (178). It is interesting to note that at that time the iceboats carried men faster than they had ever traveled before. The iceboats were much faster, in fact, than the express trains of the day.

Currier & Ives, in the light of subsequent history, indicated by their print "The American National Game of Base Ball" (80) that they had that unusual prophetic sense that was to continue throughout their entire career. Baseball at that time was not the national game that it is today, but the firm did recognize elements in the early stages of the sport that would assure the game a prominent position in the nation's sporting history. There had been baseball prints issued prior to the appearance of this one, but "The American National Game of Base Ball" was one of the first large prints produced. Although the artist of this print is unknown today, it must be said that this is one of the finest prints in the entire Currier & Ives gallery, possessing as it does an artistic quality far beyond the average of prints of the time in which it was produced.

Never in the world's history has there been a creative art firm that even closely rivaled the record of accomplishment established by Currier & Ives. In their own words, they created about "three works of art" a week for over fifty years "to meet all tastes" at the lowest possible prices. The man responsible for this great achievement was Nathaniel Currier, ably assisted by James Ives, who, by the very strength of his personality and by his business acumen, gathered together the finest artists, lithographers, and lithographic pressmen of his day to record American life graphically during the half-century that was later to be known as the Currier & Ives era.

The complete story of Currier & Ives will perhaps never be uncovered. The source of much of their material has been disclosed, and we also know how large portions of their work was obtained, but such questions as how they gathered artistic substance enough for three or four works of art a week must still remain a mystery. As time goes on, these problems may possibly be solved. It is enough at present that we recognize the rich legacy that has been handed down to us by Currier & Ives in the complete story in pictures of nearly threescore of the most exciting and robust years America has ever known.

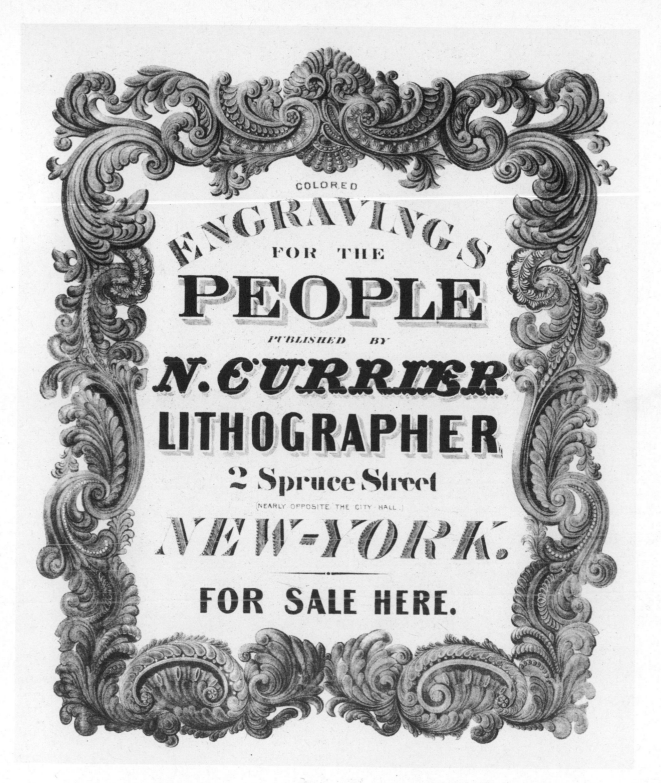

COLORED

ENGRAVINGS
FOR THE
PEOPLE
PUBLISHED BY
N. CURRIER
LITHOGRAPHER
2 Spruce Street
(NEARLY OPPOSITE THE CITY-HALL.)
NEW-YORK.
FOR SALE HERE.

PLATE 5

THE SAILOR'S RETURN.

Lith & Pub by J Currer 2 Spruce St. H.

THE SAILORS ADIEU.

Lith & Pub by N Currer 2 Spruce Street N.Y.

PLATE 6

SOLDIER'S RETURN.

OFF FOR THE WAR,

THE SOLDIER'S ADIEU!

PLATE 7

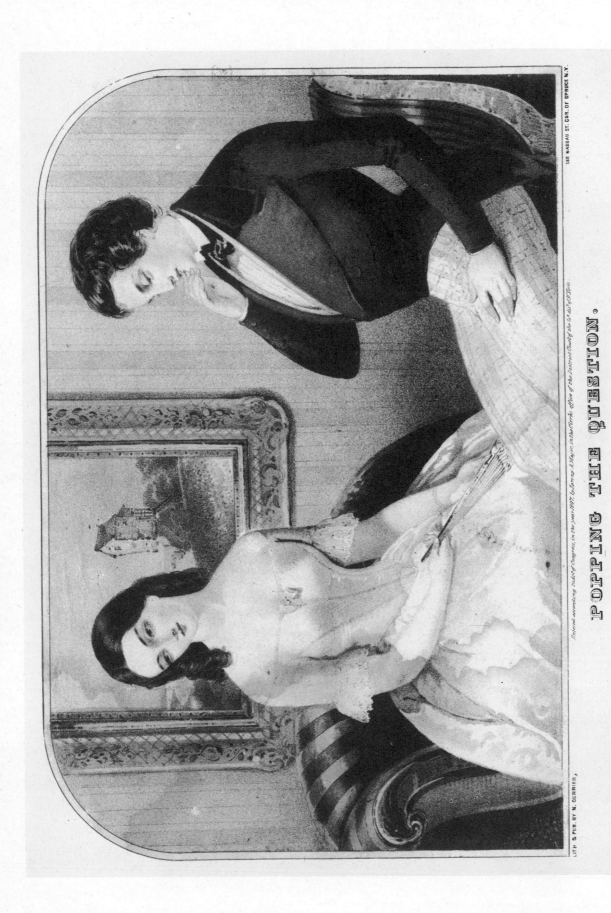

LITH & PUB. BY N. CURRIER,

152 NASSAU ST. COR. OF SPRUCE N.Y.

POPPING THE QUESTION.

Entered according to Act of Congress, in the year 1847, by Currier & Mayer, in the Clerk's office of the District Court, for the Sd. of New York

PLATE 8

PEYTONA AND FASHION.

IN THEIR GREAT MATCH FOR $20,000.

OVER THE UNION COURSE L.I. MAY 13TH 1845, WON BY PEYTONA.

Time 7: 39¾ 7: 45¼

PLATE 9

THE LIFE OF A HUNTER.
"A tight fix"

PLATE 10

THE LOVERS QUARREL.

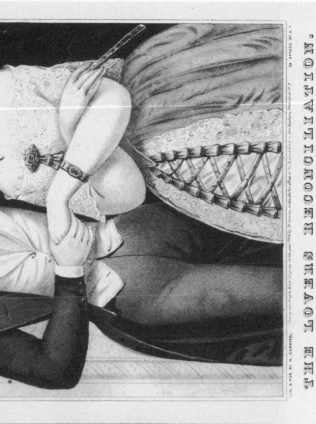

THE LOVERS RECONCILLIATION.

PLATE 11

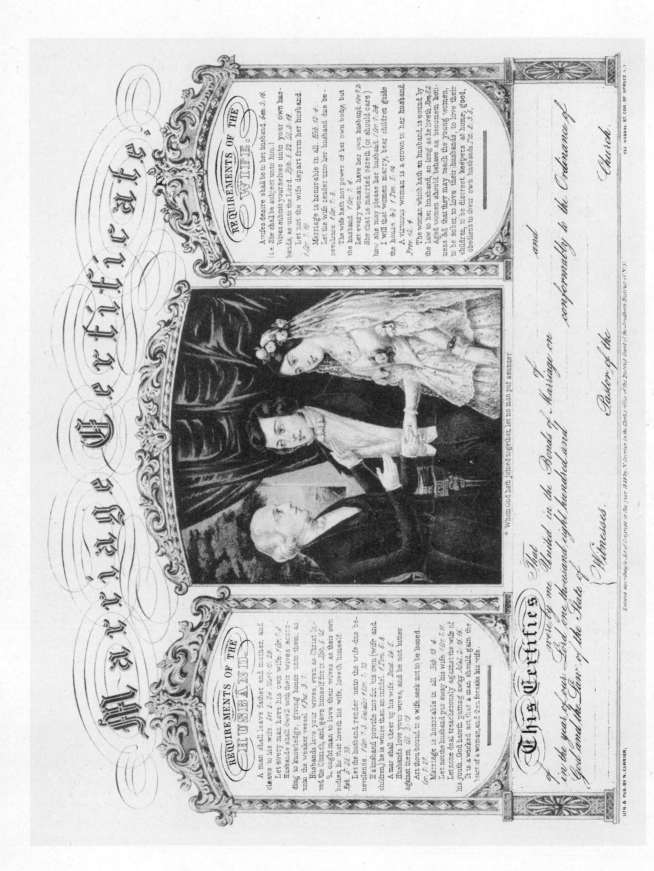

PLATE 12

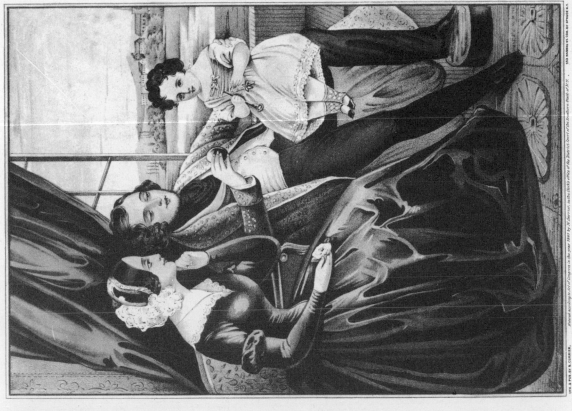

MARRIED.

SINGLE.

PLATE 13

JOHN A.ROEBLING,ESQ. ENGINEER.

C. PARSONS, DEL.

Entered according to Act of Congress in the year 1856 by N.Currier, in the Clerks Office of the District Court of the Southern District of N.Y.

THE RAIL ROAD SUSPENSION BRIDGE.

NEAR NIAGARA FALLS.

Length of Bridge 822 feet. Height above Water 240 feet.

NEW YORK, PUBLISHED BY CURRIER & IVES 152 NASSAU STREET.

PLATE 14

CATCHING A TROUT.

"We hab you now, sar"

NEW YORK, PUBLISHED BY N. CURRIER, 152 NASSAU STREET.

PLATE 15

PLATE 16

AMERICAN FIELD SPORTS.

"Flush'd"

NEW YORK PUBLISHED BY CURRIER & IVES, 152 NASSAU STREET

PLATE 17

ENGLISH SNIPE.

PRAIRIE HENS.

PLATE 18

THE "LIGHTNING EXPRESS" TRAINS.

"Leaving the Junction"

NEW YORK PUBLISHED BY CURRIER & IVES, 152 NASSAU STREET

PLATE 19

THE WRECK OF THE STEAM SHIP "SAN FRANCISCO".

PLATE 20

LEXINGTON

Awful Conflagration of the Steam Boat LEXINGTON In Long Island Sound on Monday Eve'g Jan'y 13th 1840 by which melancholy occurrence over 100 PERSONS PERISHED

PLATE 21

PLATE 22

PUBLISHED BY CURRIER & IVES   COPYRIGHT 1890 BY CURRIER & IVES, N.Y.   115 NASSAU ST. NEW YORK

A HOWLING SWELL - ON THE WAR PATH,

Aw! I say Billay! pour us a snifter, and bring on your Injuns!"

PUBLISHED BY CURRIER & IVES   COPYRIGHT 1890 BY CURRIER & IVES, N.Y.   115 NASSAU ST. NEW YORK

A HOWLING SWELL - WITH HIS SCALP IN DANGER.

"Aw! I dont want to hunt Injuns anymore, I want to go home!"

PLATE 23

PLATE 24

A MULE TRAIN ON AN UP GRADE.

"GOLLY! WHERE IS DIS YERE PROMIS LAND."

A MULE TRAIN ON A DOWN GRADE.

"CLAR DE TRACK FOR WE'S A COMIN."

PLATE 25

Copyright, 1876 by Currier & Ives, New York.

FRANKLIN'S EXPERIMENT, JUNE 1752.

Demonstrating the identity of Lightning and Electricity, from which he invented the Lightning Rod.

Lith. & Pub. by N. Currier,

2 Spruce St. N. Y.

SHAKERS NEAR LEBANON.

PLATE 26

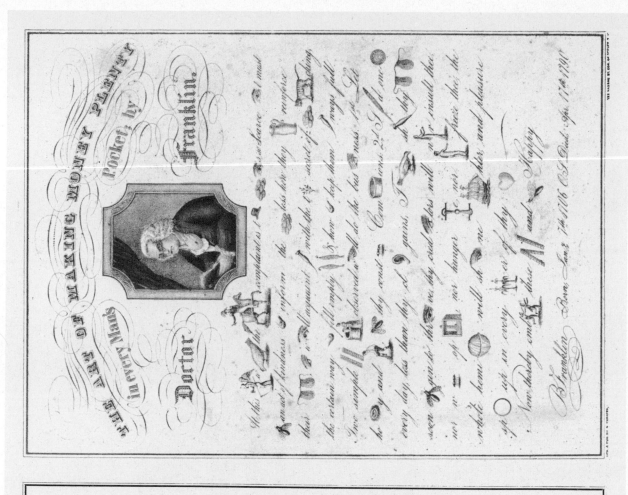

THE ART OF MAKING MONEY PLENTY

IN EVERY MAN'S POCKET

BY

DOCTOR FRANKLIN

At this time when the general complaint is that money is so scarce it must be an act of kindness to inform the moneyless how they can reinforce their purses. I will acquaint all with the true secret of money catching, the certain way to fill empty purses & how to keep them always full. Two simple rules well observed will do the business. 1st Let honesty and labor be thy constant companions: 2d Spend one penny every day less than thy clear gains: Then shall thy purses soon begin to thrive, thy creditors will never insult thee nor want oppress nor hunger bite, nor naked freeze thee, the whole hemisphere will shine brighter, and pleasure spring up in every corner of thy heart.

Now thereby embrace these rules and be happy.

B. Franklin. Born Jany. 7th, 1706, O.S. Died Apr. 17th, 1790

PLATE 27

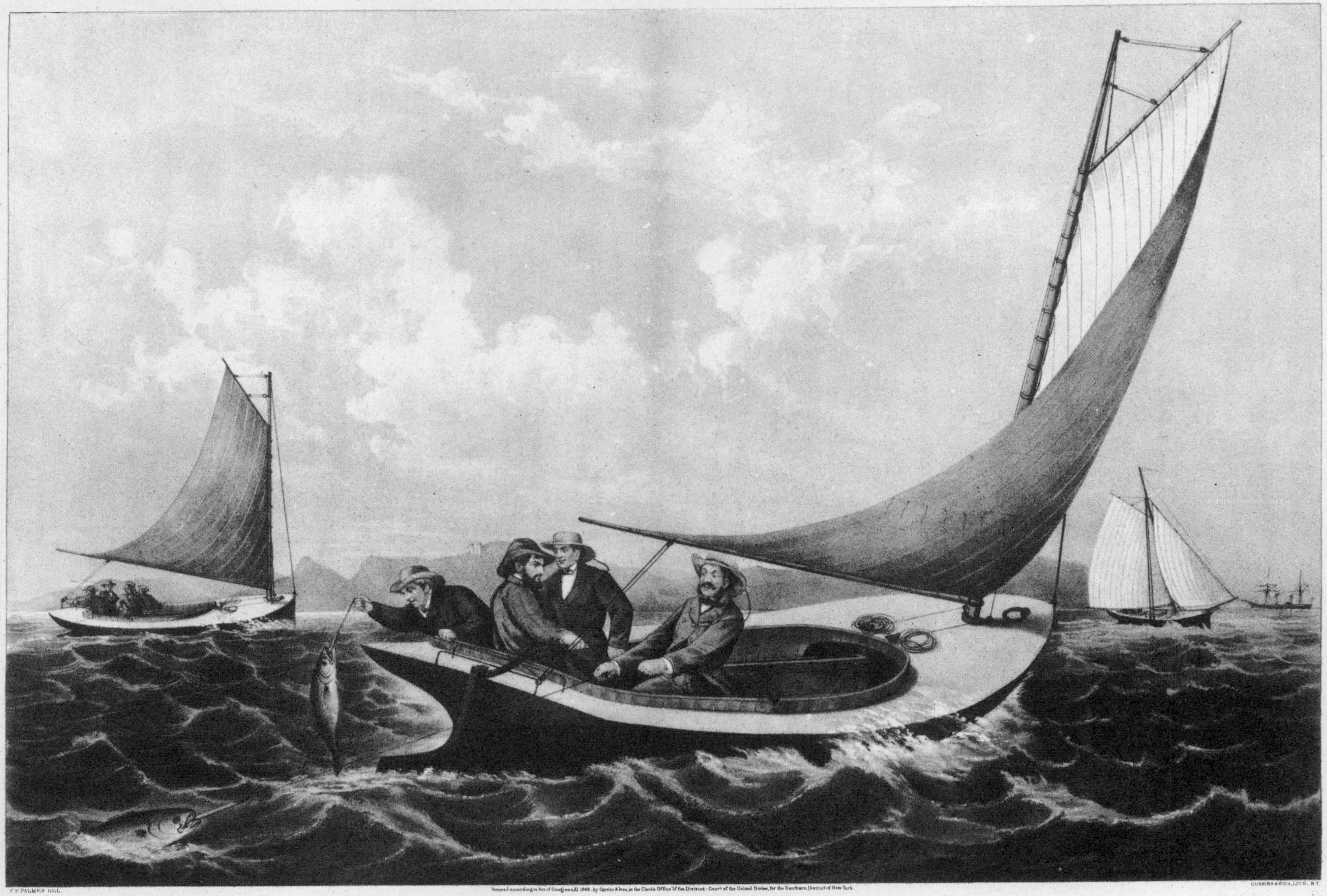

F. F. PALMER DEL.

Entered according to Act of Congress A.D. 1866, by Currier & Ives, in the Clerk's Office of the District Court of the United States, for the Southern District of New York.

CURRIER & IVES, LITH. N.Y.

TROLLING FOR BLUE FISH.

NEW YORK, PUBLISHED BY CURRIER & IVES, 152 NASSAU STREET.

PLATE 28

LIFE ON THE PRAIRIE.
The Buffalo Hunt

PLATE 29

WINTER IN THE COUNTRY.

Getting Ice.

NEW-YORK, PUBLISHED BY CURRIER & IVES. 152 NASSAU STREET.

PLATE 30

PREPARING FOR MARKET.

PLATE 31

THE DANGER SIGNAL.

PLATE 32

HARVEST.

PLATE 33

"HIGH WATER" IN THE MISSISSIPPI.

PLATE 34.

THE MAMMOTH IRON STEAM-SHIP "GREAT EASTERN" 22,500 TONS, 3000 HORSE POWER.

LENGTH 680 FT (OVER ⅛ OF A MILE.)
BREADTH 83 FT
FOUR DECKS.
18,915 TONS REGISTER.
5000 TONS LARGER THAN NOAH'S ARK.
DRAUGHT OF WATER 20 FT
& WHEN LADEN 30 FT

Designed by J. K. Brunel, Esq. F.R.S. Built by Messrs Scott Russell, London. Weight of Iron used in the construction 10,000 Tons. Combined Steam-power 3000 horses & spreads 6,500 square Yards of canvas. To walk round the Deck exceeds ⅓ of a mile.

DIAMETER OF SIDE WHEELS 60 FT
DIAMETER OF SCREW PROPELLER 24 FT
DEPTH FROM DECK TO HOLD 60 FT
WILL CARRY 10,000 TROOPS OR
800 FIRST CLASS
2000 SECOND D° } Total 4000.
1200 THIRD D°

152 NASSAU ST NEW Y.

PLATE 35

Lith. & Pub. by N. Currier.

2 Spruce St. N. Y.

QUEEN OF THE AMAZONS ATTACKED BY A LION.

PLATE 36

CORNWALLIS IS TAKEN!

Lieut. Col. Tilghman of Washington's staff, announcing the surrender of Cornwallis, from the steps of the State House (Independence Hall) at midnight, October 23rd 1781.

BAPTURE OF ANDRE 1780.

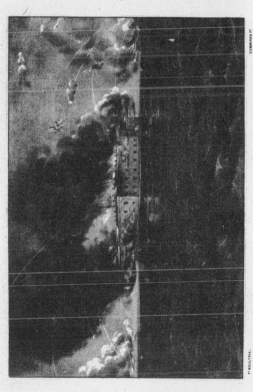

BOMBARDMENT OF FORT SUMTER, CHARLESTON HARBOR.
12th & 13th of April, 1861.

THE FALL OF RICHMOND VA ON THE NIGHT OF APRIL 2nd 1865.

PLATE 37

UTH. & PUB. BY N. CURRIER,

Entered according to Act of Congress in the year 1849 by N. Currier, in the Clerks office of the District Court of the Southern District of N.Y.

152 NASSAU ST. COR. OF SPRUCE N.Y.

THE STAR OF THE ROAD.

PLATE 38

LANDSCAPE, FRUIT AND FLOWERS.

PLATE 39

THE ROCKY MOUNTAINS.

EMIGRANTS CROSSING THE PLAINS.

NEW YORK, PUBLISHED BY CURRIER & IVES, 152 NASSAU ST.

PLATE 40

MINER, STEVENS & CO.

MANUFACTURERS OF

FIRST CLASS CARRIAGES AND LIGHT WAGONS,

WAREROOMS, No. 656 BROADWAY;

PLATE 41

THE FLOWER GIRL.

JULIA.

PLATE 42

STEAMBOAT RACE ON THE MISSISSIPPI.
ACT IV. SCENE III.
JARRETT & PALMER'S REVIVAL OF UNCLE TOM'S CABIN.

PLATE 43

PLATE 44

FASHIONABLE TURN-OUTS" IN CENTRAL PARK.

NEW YORK, PUBLISHED BY CURRIER & IVES 152 NASSAU STREET.

PLATE 45

HIGHLAND FLING.

LITH. & PUB. BY N. CURRIER.

Entered according to Act of Congress A.D. 1846 by N. Currier in the Clerks Office of the District Court of the Southern District of N.Y.

152 NASSAU St. Cor. of Spruce N.Y.

PLATE 46

MARION'S BRIGADE CROSSING THE PEDEE RIVER, S.C. 1778.

ON THEIR WAY TO ATTACK THE BRITISH FORCE UNDER TARLETON.

PLATE 47

ISABELLA.

EMELINE.

PLATE 48

"HUSKING."

PLATE 49

MINK TRAPPING.

"Prime"

PLATE 50

FROM NATURE AND ON STONE BY F. F. PALMER.   Entered according to Act of Congress, in the year 1852, by N. Currier, in the Clerk's Office, of the District Court of the Southern District of N.Y.   LITH. OF CURRIER & IVES, N. Y.

NEW YORK, PUB. BY CURRIER & IVES, 152 NASSAU STREET.

T H E   T R O U T   S T R E A M.

PLATE 51

A CORRECT LIKENESS OF Mr H. ROCKWELL'S HORSE **ALEXANDER**, BOWERY AMPHITHEATRE, NEW YORK MARCH 17TH 1840.

Lith & Pub by N Currier 2 Spruce St. N.Y.

PLATE 52

PUBLISHED BY CURRIER & IVES

THE THATCHED COTTAGE.

125 NASSAU ST. NEW YORK.

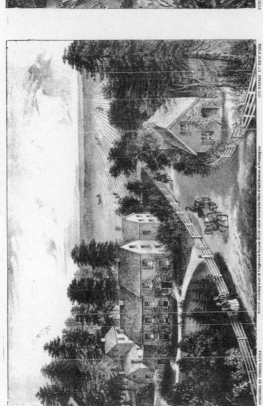

PUBLISHED BY CURRIER & IVES

THE WESTERN FARMERS HOME.

125 NASSAU ST. NEW YORK.

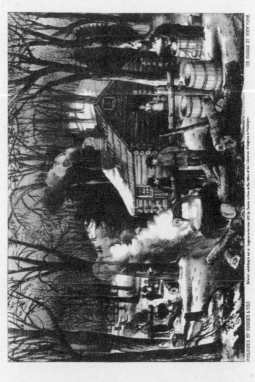

PUBLISHED BY CURRIER & IVES

MAPLE SUGARING.

EARLY SPRING IN THE NORTHERN WOODS.

125 NASSAU ST. NEW YORK.

PUBLISHED BY CURRIER & IVES

FROZEN UP.

125 NASSAU ST. NEW YORK.

PLATE 53

PUBLISHED BY CURRIER & IVES

Entered according to act of Congress in the year 1872 by Currier & Ives in the Office of the Librarian of Congress at Washington.

125 NASSAU ST NEW YORK

THE PUZZLED FOX.

Find the Horse, Lamb, Wild Boar, Mens and Womens Faces.

PLATE 54

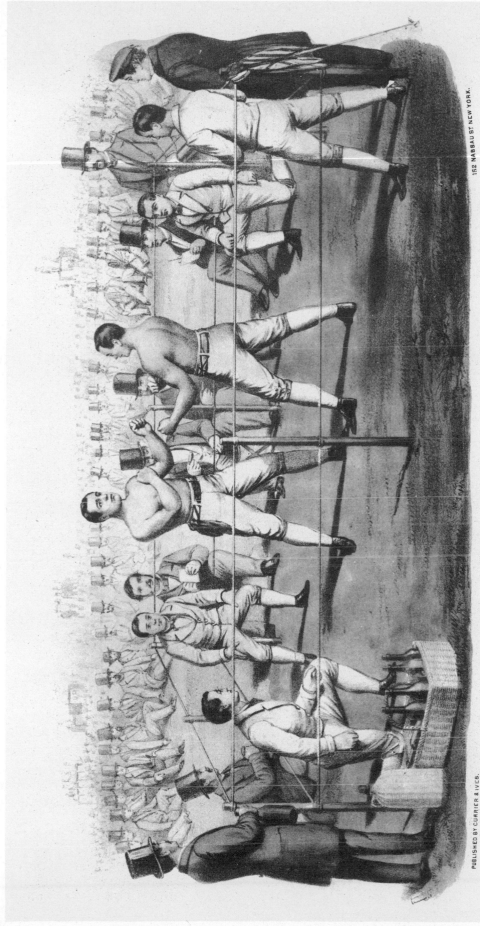

152 NASSAU ST NEW YORK.

THE GREAT FIGHT FOR THE CHAMPIONSHIP.

BETWEEN JOHN C. HEENAN "THE BENICIA BOY", & TOM SAYERS "CHAMPION OF ENGLAND".

Which took place April 17th 1860, at Farnborough, England.

THE BATTLE LASTED 2 HOURS 20 MINUTES 42 ROUNDS, WHEN THE MOB RUSHED IN & ENDED THE FIGHT.

HEENAN stands 6 ft 1½ in, fighting weight 190 lbs. Born May 2nd 1835.   SAYERS stands 5 ft 8 in, fighting wt 150 lbs. Born 1826.

PLATE 55

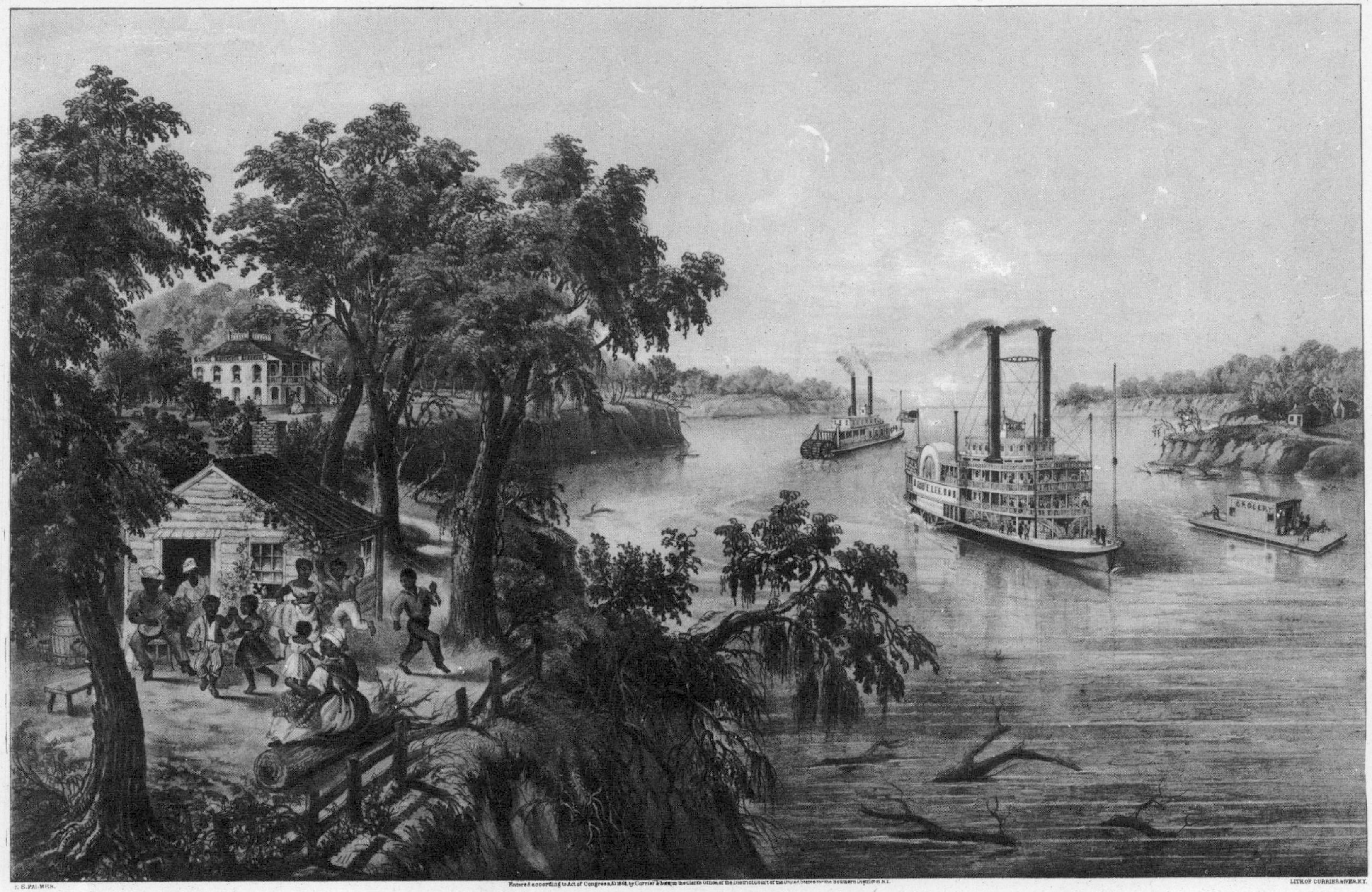

F. F. PALMER. Entered according to Act of Congress, A.D. 1868, by Currier & Ives, in the Clerk's Office, of the District Court of the United States for the Southern District of N.Y. LITH. OF CURRIER & IVES, N.Y.

LOW WATER IN THE MISSISSIPPI.

NEW YORK, PUBLISHED BY CURRIER & IVES, 115 NASSAU ST

PLATE 56

FLORA TEMPLE.

PLATE 57

PLATE 58

PLATE 59

THE WHALE FISHERY.

THE SPERM WHALE "IN A FLURRY".

NEW YORK. PUBL BY CURRIER & IVES. 152 NASSAU ST.

PLATE 60

THE CELEBRATED HORSE DEXTER, "THE KING OF THE TURF"

IN HIS GREAT MATCH AGAINST TIME OCT. 18TH 1865.

TROTTING A MILE UNDER THE SADDLE, IN THE UNPRECEDENTED TIME OF: 2:18¼

DEXTER IS A BROWN GELDING, 15 HANDS 1 INCH HIGH, FOALED IN 1858 SIRED
BY RYSDYK'S HAMBLETONIAN, DAM HAWKIN'S MARE BY AMERICAN STAR,
HE WAS RAISED BY JONATHAN HAWKINS, MONTGOMERY, ORANGE CO., N.Y.

AT THE BUFFALO N.Y. FAIR GROUNDS, AUG.28TH 1866, IN A RACE TO SADDLE, AGAINST GENERAL BUTLER,
MILE HEATS BEST 3 IN 5, DEXTER WON IN THREE STRAIGHT HEATS, TROTTING THE THIRD HEAT IN 2:16!!!
AND THE LAST HALF MILE IN 1:06!!!

FASHION COURSE, L. I., OCT. 16TH 1865.
E.V. W. SNEDEKER WAGERED $3000, TO 1000, THAT THE HORSE DEXTER
TROTTING A MILE COULD NOT BEAT V MIN IN SEC. H. WOODRUFF ENTERED DEXTER
HORSE DEXTER RIDDEN BY JOHN MURPHY, 145 LB. WON   TIME, 2:18⅛
FASHION COURSE, L.I. OCT. 27TH 1865, MATCH $2000, 2 MILE HEATS TO WAGON.
H. WOODRUFF'S, BR.G. DEXTER,   1 1
B. TALMAN'S, BLK.G. GEN.L BUTLER,   2 2
Time 5:00¼ 4:56¼.

AVON SPRINGS, N.Y. HALF MILE TRACK, AUG. 6TH 1866, PURSE $ 1000.,
MILE HEATS IN HARNESS.
H. WOODRUFF'S, BR.G. DEXTER,   1 1
J. L.ROFF'S, JR. GEO. M. PATCHEN,   2 2
Time, 2:31½ 2:21.

PLATE 61

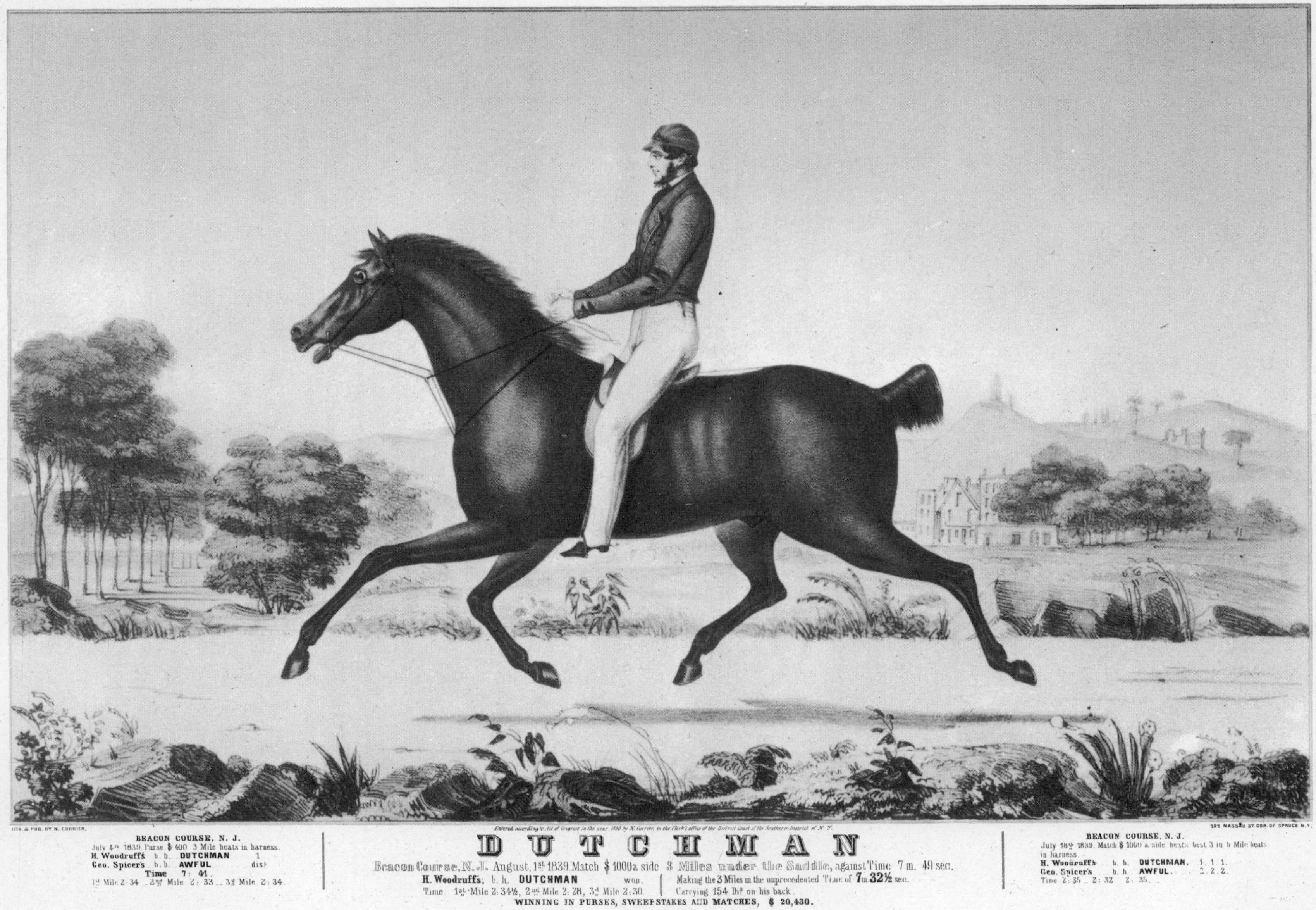
LITH. & PUB. BY N. CURRIER,
152 NASSAU ST. COR. OF SPRUCE N.Y.
DUTCHMAN
Beacon Course, N. J. August, 1st 1839. Match $ 1000 a side 3 Miles under the Saddle, against Time 7 m. 49 sec.
H. Woodruff's, b. h. DUTCHMAN won.
Time 1st Mile 2:34½, 2nd Mile 2:28, 3d Mile 2:30.
Making the 3 Miles in the unprecedented Time of 7m. 32½ sec.
Carrying 154 lbs on his back.
WINNING IN PURSES, SWEEPSTAKES AND MATCHES, $ 20,430.
BEACON COURSE, N. J.
July 4th 1839. Purse $ 400 3 Mile heats in harness.
H. Woodruff's b. h. DUTCHMAN 1
Geo. Spicer's b. h. AWFUL dist
Time 7: 41.
1st Mile 2: 34 .. 2nd Mile 2: 33 .. 3d Mile 2: 34.
BEACON COURSE, N. J.
July 18th 1839. Match $ 1000 a side heats best 3 in 5 Mile heats in harness.
H. Woodruff's b. h. DUTCHMAN. 1. 1. 1.
Geo. Spicer's b. h. AWFUL. 2. 2. 2.
Time 2: 35 .. 2: 32 2: 35.

PLATE 62

PUBLISHED BY CURRIER & IVES.

"A CLEARING."

PUB. BY CURRIER & IVES.

A SUBURBAN RETREAT.

PUB. BY CURRIER & IVES.

HUDSON RIVER—CROW NEST.

PUBLISHED BY CURRIER & IVES.

HOME SWEET HOME.

PLATE 63

THE OLD STONE HOUSE. L. I. 1699.

LITH. & PUB. BY N. CURRIER, 152 NASSAU STREET N. Y.

Plate 64

AN AMERICAN RAILWAY SCENE, AT HORNELLSVILLE, ERIE RAILWAY.

THE GREAT TRUNK LINE AND UNITED STATES MAIL ROUTE between New York City and the Western States and Territories, renowned for its Beautiful Scenery, its substantial road bed. DOUBLE TRACKED with steel rail, and its well appointed Passenger trains, equipped with the celebrated Pullman Hotel, Drawing Room and Sleeping Coaches.

PLATE 65

PLATE 66

CENTRAL PARK IN WINTER.

PLATE 67

PUBLISHED BY CURRIER & IVES.

SNOWED UP.

RUFFED GROUSE IN WINTER.

Entered according to Act of Congress in 1867 by Currier & Ives, in the Clerk's Office of the District Court of the United States, for the Southern District of N.Y.

PLATE 68

FROM NATURE AND ON STONE BY F. F. PALMER

LITH. OF N. CURRIER, N.Y.

WOODCOCK SHOOTING.

PUBLISHED BY N CURRIER, 152 NASSAU ST NEW YORK.

PLATE 69

AMERICAN EXPRESS TRAIN.

NEW YORK, PUBLISHED BY CURRIER & IVES, 152 NASSAU ST

PLATE 70

MOUNT WASHINGTON AND THE WHITE MOUNTAINS,

FROM THE VALLEY OF CONWAY.

PLATE 71

GREAT CONFLAGRATION AT PITTSBURGH PA.

APRIL 10ᵗʰ 1845

Nearly 1200 houses destroyed, — estimated loss of Property $ 9,000,000.

Pub. by Turner & Fisher 15 North, 6ᵗʰ Street Philᵃ & N. Carrier N.Y.

PLATE 72

125 NASSAU ST. NEW YORK.

THE BIRTH-PLACE OF WASHINGTON.

At Bridges Creek, Westmoreland Co. Va. (Feby. 22nd 1732.)

This House commanded a view of the Potomac, and the opposite shore of Maryland. The roof was steep, and sloped down into low projecting eaves. It had four rooms on the ground floor, and others in the attic, and an immense chimney at each end.

PLATE 73

NORTHERN SCENERY.

SILVER CASCADE

THE RIVER ROAD.

AMONG THE HILLS.

PUBLISHED BY CURRIER & IVES.   125 NASSAU ST. NEW YORK

GEMS OF AMERICAN SCENERY.

Plate 74

WOODCOCK SHOOTING.

SHOOTING ON THE PRAIRIE.

BEAR HUNTING.
CLOSE QUARTERS.

WOOD-DUCKS.

PLATE 75

THE GREAT OCEAN YACHT RACE.

BETWEEN THE HENRIETTA, FLEETWING & VESTA.

THE "GOOD BYE" TO THE YACHT CLUB STEAMER "RIVER QUEEN," 4 MILES EAST OF SANDY HOOK LIGHT SHIP. DEC. 11TH 1866.

The HENRIETTA arrived off the Needles, Isle of Wight, England at 3.45 P.M. Dec. 25th 1866, winning the Race and making the run in 13 days 22 hours. mean time.
The FLEETWING arrived 8 hours afterwards, and the VESTA 1¾ hours after the Fleetwing.

PLATE 76

THE MAN THAT GAVE BARNUM HIS "TURN".

BEFORE.

AFTER.

PLATE 77

PLATE 78

"TROTTING CRACKS" AT THE FORGE.

MOUNTAIN BOY
GREY EAGLE
LADY THORN

PLATE 79

THE AMERICAN NATIONAL GAME OF BASE BALL.

GRAND MATCH FOR THE CHAMPIONSHIP AT THE ELYSIAN FIELDS, HOBOKEN, N. J.

PLATE 80

BRANDING SLAVES,

ON THE COAST OF AFRICA PREVIOUS TO EMBARKATION.

PLATE 81

ROBINSON CRUSOE AND HIS PETS.

It would have made a stoic smile to have seen me and my little family, how like a King I walked attended by my servants; Poll to talk to me my Dog, Cats, Kittens Goats and Kids, all clustering around me as if each one desired a word of recognition and affection.

NOAH'S ARK.

Of clean beasts, and of beasts that are not clean, and of fowls and of every thing that creepeth upon the earth, there went in two and two unto Noah into the Ark, the male and the female, as God had commanded Noah. Gen. Chap. 8 & 9 v.

PLATE 82

MY FIRST LOVE.

Lith. & Pub. by N. Currier. 2 S! New York.

PLATE 83

RUINS OF THE MERCHANT'S EXCHANGE N. Y.

After the Destructive Conflagration of Dec.r 16 & 17 1835.

Sketched and drawn on Stone by J.H.Bufford.

Published by J.Disturnell, 156 Broad Way, & of H.Bufford. 10.Beekman St.

Entered according to Act of Congress by J.H.Bufford in the Clerk's Office of the Southern District of N.Y. 1836.

Printed by . V. Currier 1 Wall St. N. York   *On Stone by J. G. Bufford*

RUINS OF THE PLANTERS HOTEL, NEW-ORLEANS,

Which fell at two O'Clock, on the Morning of the 15th of May 1835, burying 50 persons, 40 of which escaped with their lives.—

PLATE 84

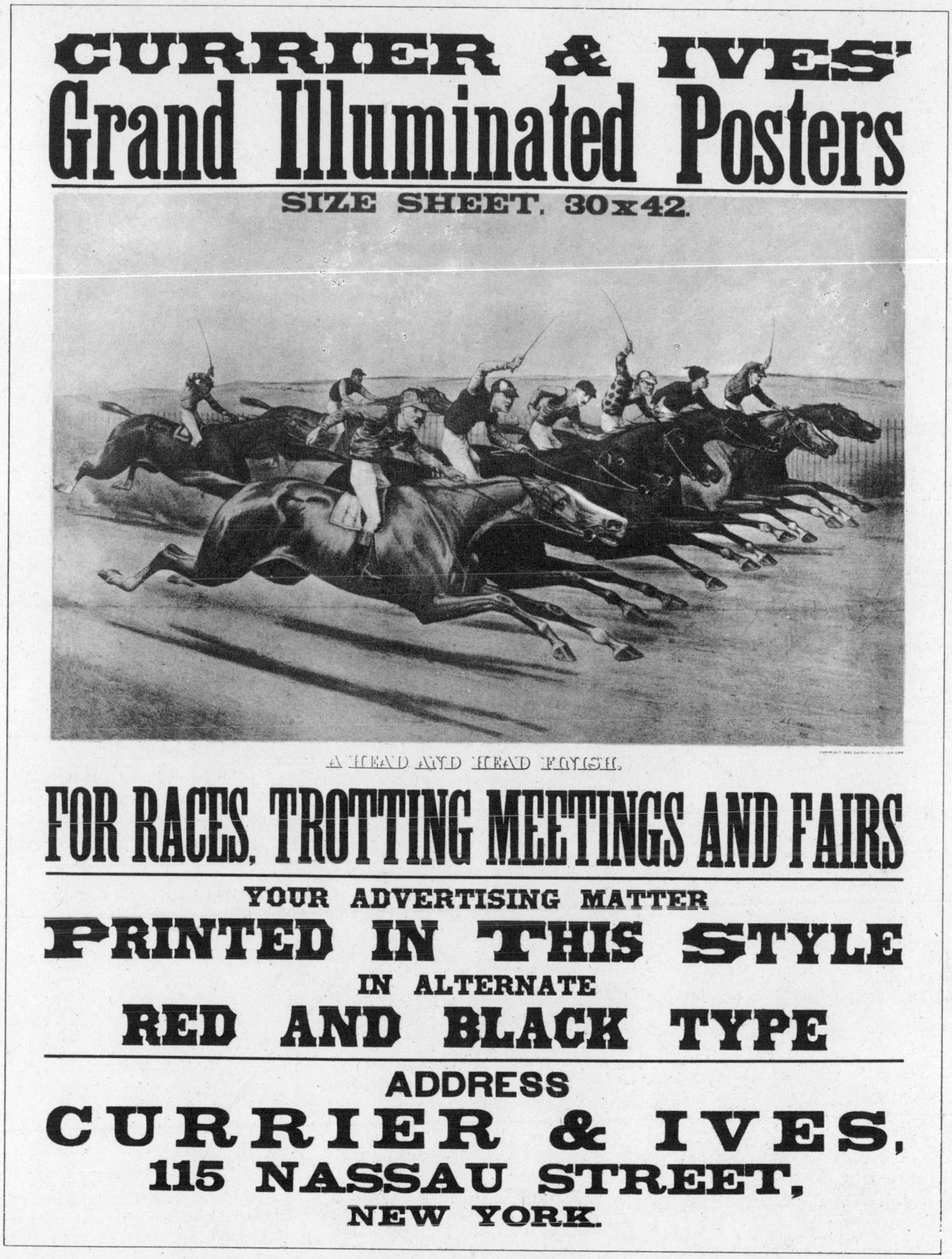
CURRIER & IVES'
Grand Illuminated Posters
SIZE SHEET, 30x42.
A HEAD AND HEAD FINISH.
FOR RACES, TROTTING MEETINGS AND FAIRS
YOUR ADVERTISING MATTER
PRINTED IN THIS STYLE
IN ALTERNATE
RED AND BLACK TYPE
ADDRESS
CURRIER & IVES,
115 NASSAU STREET,
NEW YORK.

PLATE 85

THE TREE OF LIFE. ✦ THE CHRISTIAN.

"Even so every good tree bringeth forth good fruit." (Mat. VII. 17.) — "Wherefore by their fruits ye shall know them" (Mat. VII. 20.)

PLATE 86

ON THE MISSISSIPPI
LOADING COTTON.

BOUND DOWN THE RIVER.

PLATE 87

THE RUBBER.
"Put to his Trumps".

NEW YORK, PUB BY CURRIER & IVES, 152 NASSAU ST.

PLATE 88

C. PARSONS DEL.

LITH. BY B. CURRIER.

CLIPPER SHIP "NIGHTINGALE".

GETTING UNDER WEIGH OFF THE BATTERY NEW YORK.

NEW YORK PUBLISHED, BY N. CURRIER 152 NASSAU STREET

Entered according to the Act of Congress in the year 1854 by N. Currier, in the Clerk's Office of the District Court of the Southern District of N.Y.

PLATE 89

THE DRUNKARD'S PROGRESS

FROM THE FIRST GLASS TO THE GRAVE.

STEP 1.
A glass with
a Friend.

STEP 2.
A glass to
keep the
cold out.

STEP 3.
A glass
too
much.

STEP 4.
Drunk
and
riotous.

STEP 5.
The summit attained
Jolly companions
A confirmed drunkard.

STEP 6.
Poverty
and
Disease.

STEP 7.
Forsaken
by Friends

STEP 8.
Desperation and
crime.

STEP 9.
Death
by
suicide.

PLATE 90

PLATE 91

PLATE 92

OUR BOAT SETS LIGHTLY ON THE WAVE

N. Currier's Lith.

A DUET AND TRIO,

Written Composed and Arranged

and Respectfully dedicated to the

NEW YORK BOAT CLUBS,

BY

WILLIAM CLIFTON.

New-York: ATWILL. 201 Broadway.

PLATE 93

CHARTER OAK! CHARTER OAK ANCIENT AND FAIR!

N. Currier's Lith. N.Y.

AN ANCIENT AMERICAN BALLAD:

written by

M^{RS} SIGOURNEY.

the Music Composed

AND MOST RESPECTFULLY DEDICATED TO

my friend

DR JOHN D. RUSS,

(of Hartford, Con.)

by

HENRY RUSSELL.

NEW-YORK.

Published by **HEWITT & JAQUES** *239 Broadway*

PLATE 94

LITH.& PUB? BY N. CURRIER,   *Entered according to Act of Congress in the Year 1851, by N. Currier, in the Clerk's Office of the District Court of the Southern District of N.Y.*   152. NASSAU S? COR.OF SPRUCE N.Y.

THE BLOOMER COSTUME.

Plate 95

QUEEN VICTORIA.

Pub by N Currier 2 Spruce St N.Y.

PLATE 96

LITH & PUB. BY CURRIER & IVES.   152 NASSAU S? N. Y.

KISS ME QUICK.

Children: this is the third time within an hour that I have placed your hats properly upon your heads.—There !!

PLATE 97

LITH. & PUB. BY N. CURRIER,   *Entered according to Act of Congress in the year 1847 by N. Currier, in the Clerk's office of the District Court of the Southern District of New York.*   152 NASSAU ST. COR. OF SPRUCE N.Y.

THE MARRIAGE.

Plate 98

PAINTED BY JOHN TRUMBULL.

ENTERED ACCORDING TO ACT OF CONGRESS IN THE YEAR 1852 BY N. CURRIER, IN THE CLERK'S OFFICE OF THE DISTRICT COURT OF THE SOUTHERN DISTRICT OF N. Y.

LITHOGRAPHED BY N. CURRIER, N. Y.

SURRENDER OF GENERAL BURGOYNE AT SARATOGA N.Y. OCT. 17TH 1777.

PLATE 99

THE MISSISSIPPI IN TIME OF WAR.

PLATE 100

MIDNIGHT RACE ON THE MISSISSIPPI.

THROUGH THE BAYOU BY TORCHLIGHT.

PLATE 101

LITH. & PUB. BY N. CURRIER, Entered according to Act of Congress in the year 1847 by N. Currier, in the Clerks office of the District Court of the Southern District of N.Y. 152 NASSAU ST. COR. OF SPRUCE N.Y.

THE SISTERS.

Plate 102

LOOKING IN.

494.

PLATE 103

JAMES MADISON.

Fourth President of the United States.

Lith & Pub by N.Currier 2 Spruce St.N.Y.

THOMAS JEFFERSON,

Third President of the United States.

Lith & Pub by N.Currier 2 Spruce St.N.Y.

MARTIN VAN BUREN.

Eighth President of the United States.

Lith & Pub by N.Currier 2 Spruce St. N.Y.

WILLIAM HENRY HARRISON

Ninth President of the United States

Pub. by N.Currier 2 Spruce St. N.Y.

PLATE 104

GRAND DEMOCRATIC FREE SOIL BANNER.

From ─ Daguerreotypes by Plumbe.

WASHINGTON'S RECEPTION BY THE LADIES, ON PASSING THE
BRIDGE AT TRENTON, N. J. APRIL 1789.
ON HIS WAY TO NEW YORK TO BE INAUGURATED FIRST PRESIDENT OF THE UNITED STATES.

PLATE 105

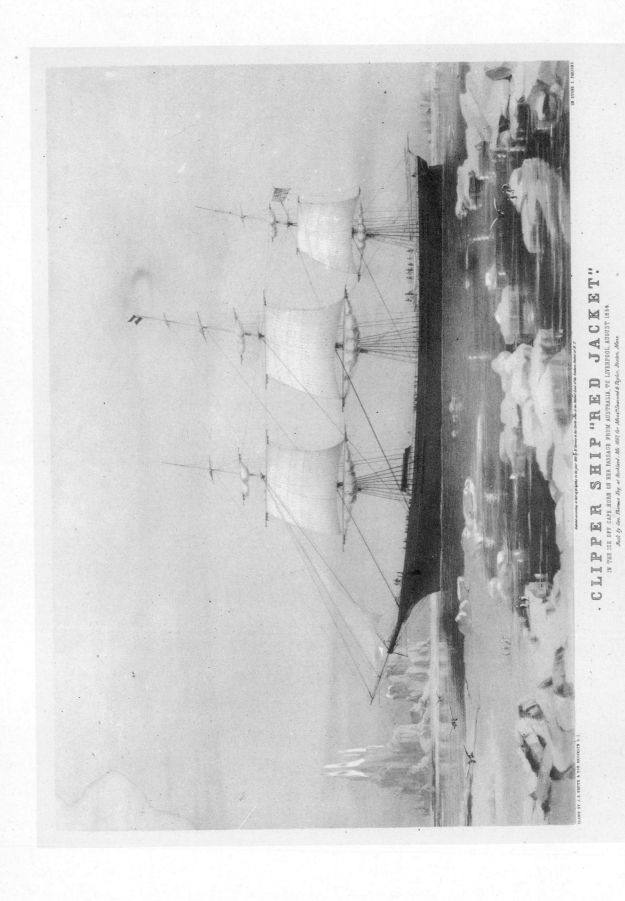

CLIPPER SHIP "RED JACKET":

IN THE ICE OFF CAPE HORN ON HER PASSAGE FROM AUSTRALIA, TO LIVERPOOL, AUGUST 1854.

Built by Geo. Thomas, Esq. at Rockland, Me 1853 &c. Messr Seacomb & Taylor, Boston, Mass

NEW YORK, PUBLISHED BY N.Y. NAGEL, 163 NASSAU STREET

PLATE 106

Entered, according to Act of Congress in the year A. 1868, by Currier & Ives in the Clerks Office of the District Court of the United States for the Southern District of New York

THE FOUR SEASONS OF LIFE: OLD AGE.

"The Season of Rest."

Last come the winter of life's ending year,
And strength departs, but love and joy abide,
That "perfect love" which "casteth out all fear."
That joy, that lives beyond life's restless tide.

Grateful for mercies past, and trusting still
In him whose goodness all our lives hath blest,
We rest secure, and calmly wait his will,
To call us hence, to his eternal rest.

NEW YORK. PUBLISHED BY CURRIER & IVES 152 NASSAU STREET

PLATE 107

FROM NATURE AND ON STONE BY F. F. PALMER   Entered according to Act of Congress in the year 1852 by N Currier, in the Patent Court of the Southern District of N.Y.   LITH OF N CURRIER, N.Y.

PARTRIDGE SHOOTING.

PUBLISHED BY N CURRIER. 152 NASSAU ST NEW YORK

Plate 108

THE HAPPY FAMILY.

RUFFED GROUSE AND YOUNG.

PLATE 109

CLIPPER SHIP DREADNOUGHT OFF TUSKAR LIGHT

PLATE 110

THE NEW YORK YACHT CLUB REGATTA.

THE START FROM THE STAKE BOAT IN THE NARROWS,

OFF THE NEW CLUB HOUSE AND GROUNDS, STATEN ISLAND. NEW YORK HARBOR.

PLATE 111

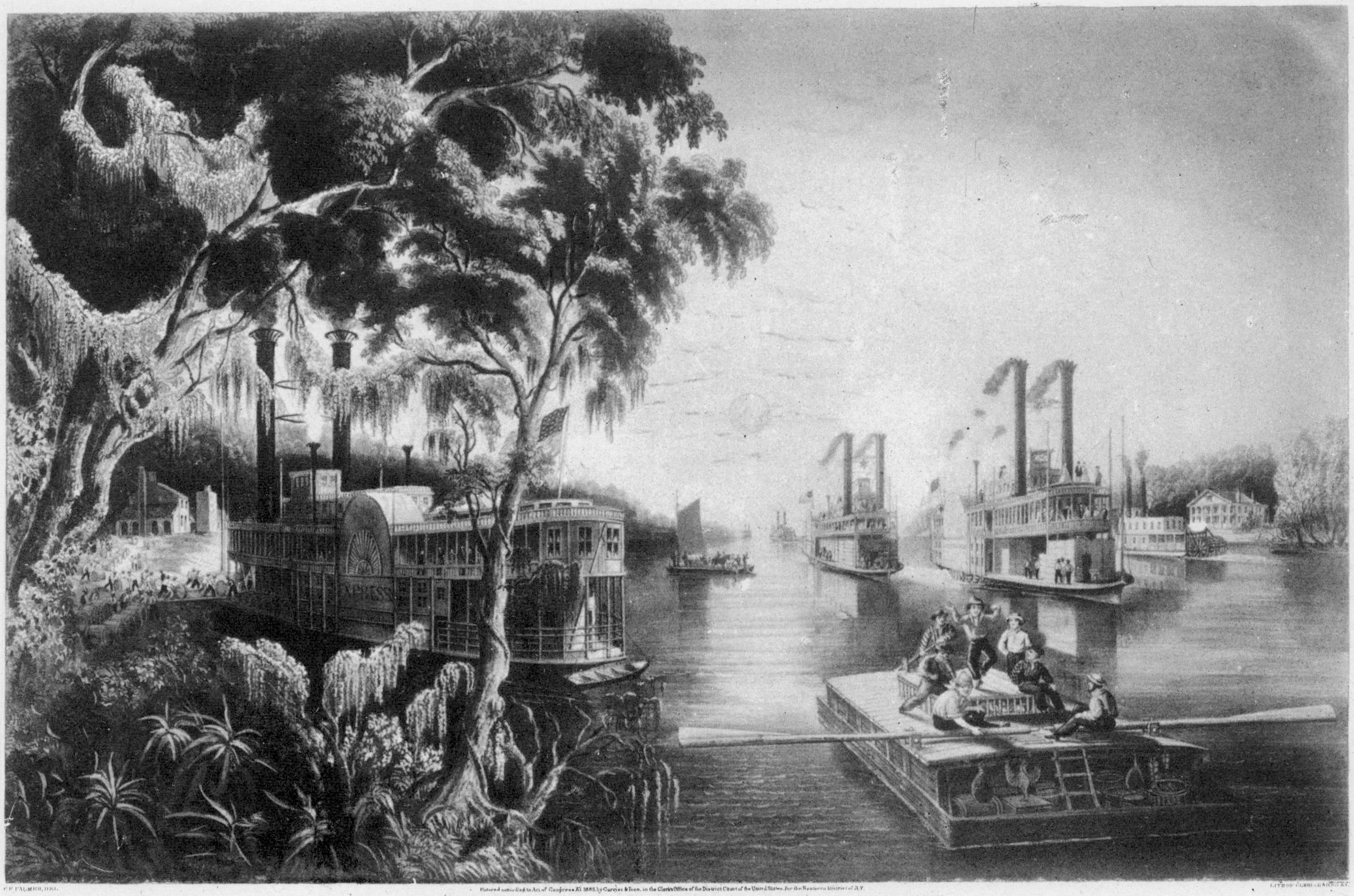

THE MISSISSIPPI IN TIME OF PEACE.

NEW YORK, PUBLISHED BY CURRIER & IVES, 152 NASSAU STREET

PLATE 112

AMERICAN FOREST SCENE

MAPLE SUGARING.

PLATE 113

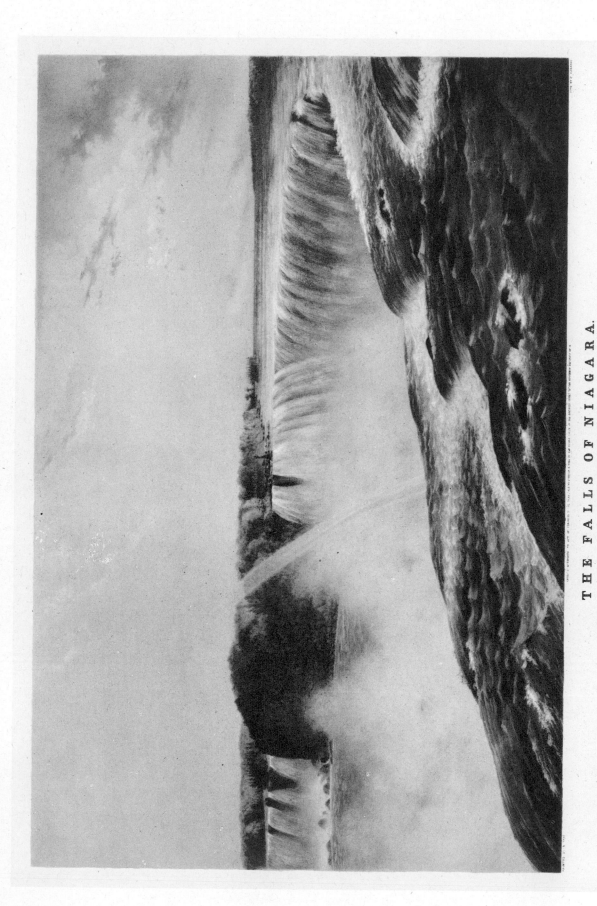

THE FALLS OF NIAGARA.

'From the Canada side'

NEW YORK PUBLISHED BY CURRIER & IVES 152 NASSAU STREET

PLATE 114

Entered according to Act of Congress AD1860 by Currier & Ives, in the Clerks Office of the District Court of the United States, for the Southern District of New York.

EARLY WINTER.

New York Published by Currier & Ives, 152 Nassau St.

PLATE 115

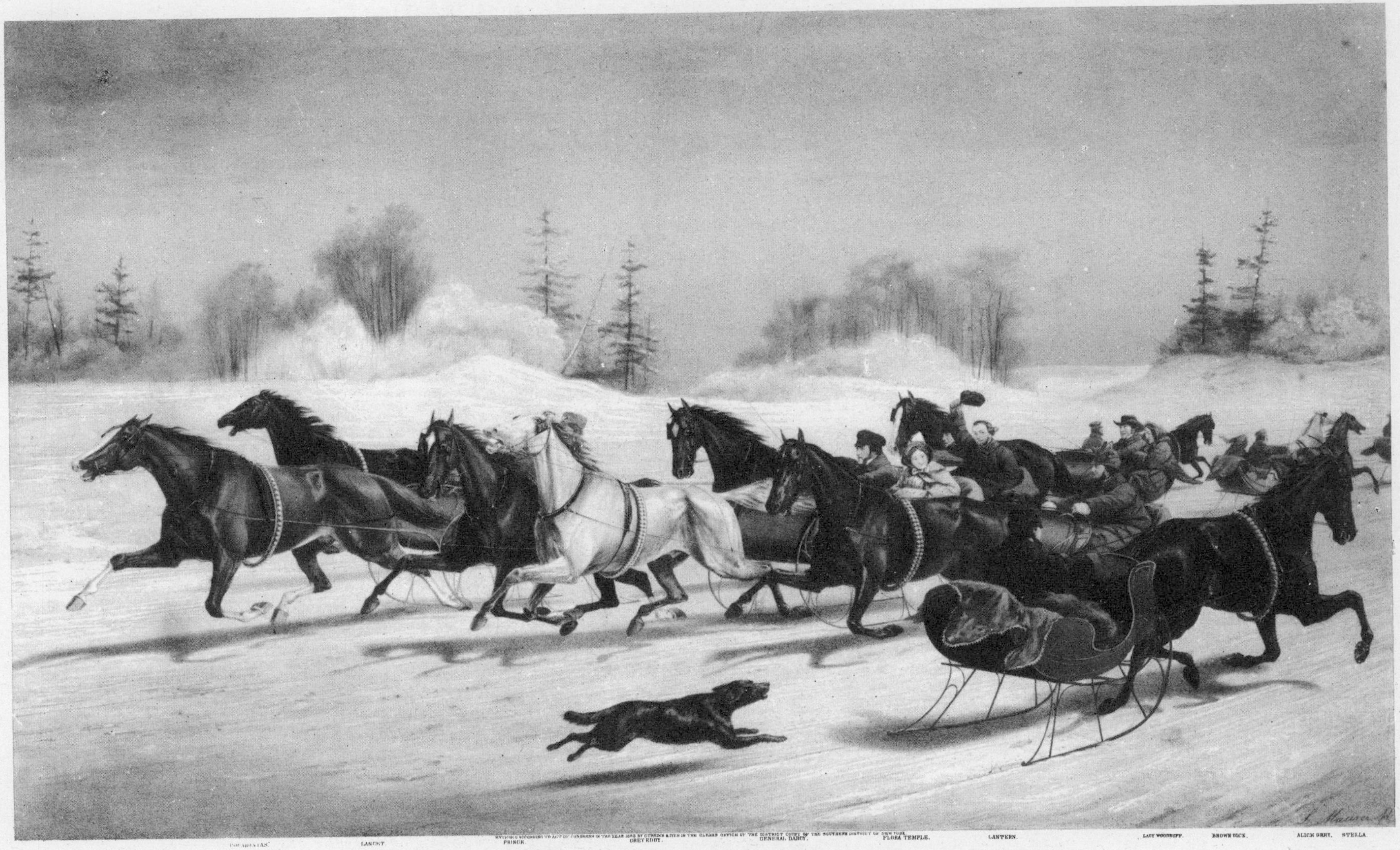

"TROTTING CRACKS ON THE SNOW."

PLATE 116

CLIPPER SHIP "COMET" OF NEW YORK.

IN A HURRICANE OFF BERMUDA, ON HER VOYAGE FROM NEW YORK TO SAN FRANCISCO, OCT. 1852.

PLATE 117

PUBLISHED BY CURRIER & IVES.   ENTERED ACCORDING TO ACT OF CONGRESS IN THE YEAR 1870 BY CURRIER & IVES IN THE OFFICE OF THE LIBRARIAN OF CONGRESS AT WASHINGTON.   152 NASSAU ST. NEW YORK.

JOHN BROWN — THE MARTYR.

Meeting a Slave Mother and her Child on the steps of Charlestown Jail, on his way to Execution.
Regarding them with a look of compassion Captain Brown stooped and kissed the Child ———— ".

THE BODY OF THE MARTYR PRESIDENT, ABRAHAM LINCOLN.

LYING IN STATE AT THE CITY HALL, N.Y. APRIL 24th & 25th 1865.

Entered according to Act of Congress A.D. 1865 by Currier & Ives, in the Clerk's Office of the District Court of the United States, for the Southern District of N.Y.

Published by Currier & Ives, 152 Nassau St N.Y.

PLATE 118

VIEW OF SAN FRANCISCO, CALIFORNIA.

TAKEN FROM TELEGRAPH HILL, APRIL 1850, BY W.ᵐ B. M.ᶜMURTRIE, DRAUGHTSMAN OF THE U.S. SURVEYING EXPEDITION.

PLATE 119

BURNING OF THE NEW YORK CRYSTAL PALACE,
on Tuesday Oct. 5th 1858.

DURING IT'S OCCUPATION FOR THE ANNUAL FAIR OF THE AMERICAN INSTITUTE.

NEW YORK, PUB'D BY CURRIER & IVES, 152 NASSAU STREET.

PLATE 120

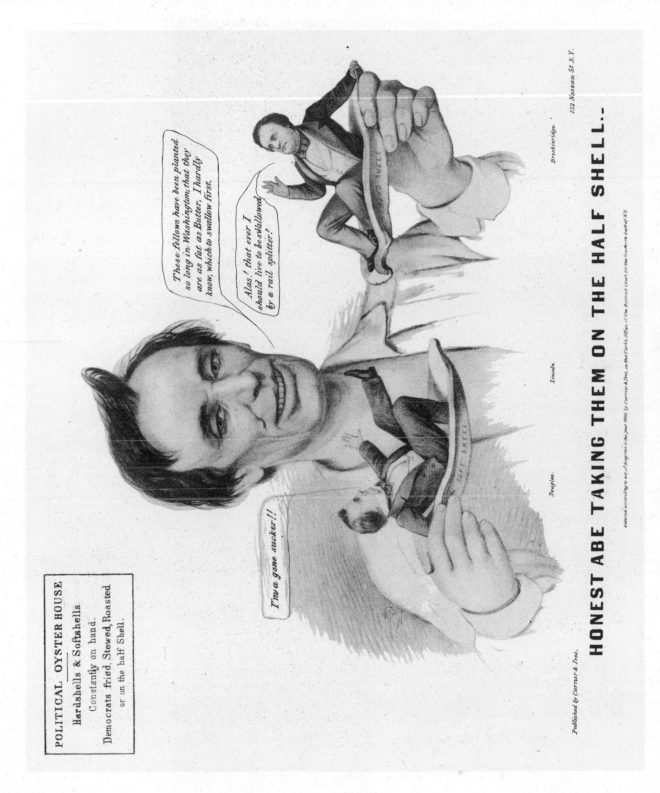

PLATE 121

PIGEON SHOOTING.

"Playing the decoy."

PLATE 122

UNCLE TOM AND LITTLE EVA.

EVA, GAYLY LAUGHING, WAS HANGING A WREATH OF ROSES ROUND HIS NECK.

"O, TOM, YOU LOOK SO FUNNY!"

LITH. & PUB. BY N. CURRIER.   152 NASSAU STREET N.Y.

THE BAD MAN AT THE HOUR OF DEATH.

The wages of Sin is Death. Rom. 6th, Ch. 23

Lo, in adapted scale of Luxury brings!   Misgive this Piece the Sinner dreads to die.
The Covetiscerate and Death's avarice Stings!   And Bids he would the King of Terror fly.

Lith. & Pub by N. Currier, 2 Spruce St. N.Y.

PLATE 123

AMERICAN WINTER SPORTS.

TROUT FISHING "ON CHATEAUGAY LAKE" (Franklin Co. N.Y.)

PLATE 124

DARTMOUTH COLLEGE.

PLATE 125

F. F. PALMER, del.

LENGTH OF KEEL .... 205 FEET
LENGTH OVER ALL .... 230 "
BREADTH OF BEAM .... 40 "
DEPTH OF HOLD .... 22 "

CLIPPER SHIP "HURRICANE"
OF NEW YORK.

NEW YORK PUBLISHED BY N. CURRIER, 152 NASSAU STREET.

Entered according to Act of Congress in the year 1851 by N Currier, in the Clerk's office of the District Court of the Southern District of N.Y.

TONS, REGISTER .... 1,608.
ISAAC C. SMITH, BUILDER.
C. W. & A. THOMAS OWNERS

LITH. BY N. CURRIER

PLATE 126

THE CHAMPIONS OF THE UNION.

152 Nassau Street. N.Y

PLATE 127

 BATTLE AT BUNKER'S HILL,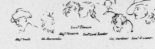

June 11th 1775.

THE BATTLE OF FAIR OAKS, Va. MAY 31st 1862.

General McClellan having advanced "The Army of the Potomac" to near Richmond, the Rebels took advantage of a terrible storm which had flooded the Valley of the Chickahominy; and at 10 O'Clock P.M. attacked the advanced lines on the right bank of the river; and succeeded in forcing them back; but Generals Heintzelman & Kearny gallantly brought up their troops and checked the enemy; while Genl Sumner by great exertions succeeded in bringing across the river, Genls Sedgewicks and Richardsons divisions; when the Rebels were driven back at the point of the bayonet, leaving over 1200 of their dead on the field. The next morning June 1st they attempted to renew the conflict but were at every point repulsed with great slaughter.

PLATE 128

PAINTED BY J. P. BUTTERSWORTH.

LITH. BY N. CURRIER N. Y.

LENGTH ON DECK .... 325 FEET.
BREADTH OF BEAM .... 53 FEET.

DEPTH OF HOLD .... 39 FEET.
TONNAGE PER REGISTER .... 4500.

Entered according to Act of Congress, in the year 1853 by N. Currier in the Clerks Office of the District Court of the Southern District N.Y.

To Donald McKay Esq. builder of the Leviathan

CLIPPER SHIP "GREAT REPUBLIC."

This print is respectfully dedicated

PLATE 129

PLAN OF GILBERT'S BALANCE FLOATING DRY DOCK
CONNECTED WITH BASIN AND RAILWAYS

IN COURSE OF CONSTRUCTION FOR THE U. S., GOV'T AT THE
Navy Yard PENSACOLA, Flor. and at the Navy Yard KITTERY, Me.

under Contract with

GILBERT & SECOR.

PLATE 130

THE ENTRANCE TO THE HIGHLANDS.

Hudson River—looking South

NEW YORK PUBLISHED BY CURRIER & IVES, 152 NASSAU STREET

Entered according to act of Congress A.D. 1864 by Currier & Ives, in the Clerks Office of the District Court of the United States for the Southern District of New York.

LITH. BY CURRIER & IVES.

PLATE 131

THE CHAMPION IN LUCK.
Dar- I know'd sumfin 'ud happen!

LAWN TENNIS AT DARKTOWN.
A Scientific Player.

THE CHAMPION IN DANGER.
Golly! he's got dis Nigga suah, less sumfin happens.

LAWN TENNIS AT DARKTOWN.
A Scientific Stroke.

PLATE 132

THE WILD WEST IN DARKTOWN.
Attack on the Deadhead Coach.

THE WILD WEST IN DARKTOWN.
The Buffalo Chase.

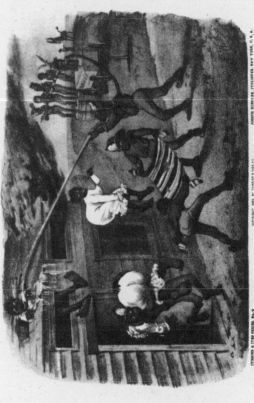

THE DARKTOWN FIRE BRIGADE—SAVED!

THE DARKTOWN FIRE BRIGADE—HOOK AND LADDER GYMNASTICS.
Brace her up dar! and cotch her on de fly!

PLATE 133

THE DARKTOWN YACHT CLUB—HARD UP FOR A BREEZE.
The cup in danger.

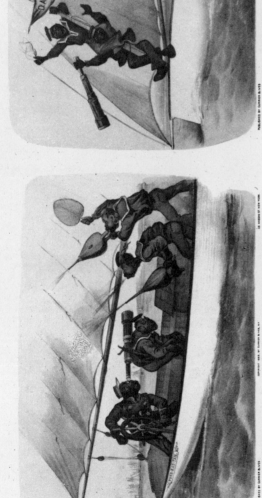

THE DARKTOWN YACHT CLUB—ON THE WINNING TACK.
The cup secure.

THE CHAMPIONS OF THE BALL RACKET.
On the Diamond Field

A BASE HIT.

PLATE 134

THE DARKTOWN HUNT - THE MEET.

"KEEP YOU TEMPERS LADIES DE ONE DAT GITS TOTHER END FUST GITS DE BRUSH."

THE DARKTOWN HUNT - PRESENTING THE BRUSH.

"YOU DONE BETTER KEEP IT KURNEL TO POLISH YOU CHEEK."

PLATE 135

Mangerton Mountain   Turk Mountain   Drooping Mountain   Glena Mountain   Tomies   Purple   Mr Billy Cuddy's Rocks   German Turk.

THE LAKES OF KILLARNEY.

1 Turk Cascade
2 Turk Cottage
3 Dinis Cottage and Island
4 Devils Island
5 Mucruss Mr Herberts M.P.
6 Mucruss Abbey
7 Brenn Fort Capt Colthurst*

8 Castle Lough D.S. Lawlers
9 Coltsmore Mr Herberts
10 South Hill Jr Leahy*
11 Flesk Cottage O'Donoghues
12 Colemans Castle
13 Capt Courtneys
14 Flesk Bridge and River.

15 Brickeen Bridge
16 Mucruss Mines
17 Glena Cottage
18 Derkyn Garden
19 O'Sullivans Cascade
20 Ross Mines and Furnace
21 Ross Castle and Bridge

22 Flesk Cottage McCann's
23 Park House Earl Cousins
24 Wood Lawn Rt Hon Wm Browns
25 Earl Kenmares
26 Killarney Town
27 Benn House
28 O'Donoghues Prison

29 Mouse Island
30 Innisfallen Abbey and Cottage
31 Stag Hunt
32 Brown or Burnt Island
33 Heron Island
34 Lamb Island
35 Victoria Hotel

36 Belle View Earl Kenmares
37 Prospect Hall Rt Hon Capt Brown's
38 Paddock Christopher Galwey's
39 Dunagh River
40 The Race Course
41 Mahony's Point
42 Lake View James O'Connell's

43 Oreagh Jn O'Connell's
44 O'Sullivan's Tomies
45 Dunlo Castle Major Mahony's
46 Hare Hunt
47 Benn Fort Person Mullins
48 Leune River
49 Aghadoe Abbey and Tower

50 Madam O'Donoghues
51 Lady Headly's Aghadoe
52 Ten and Chicken
53 Dunlo Castle Major Mahony's
54 Upper Lake
55 Old Weir Bridge
55 Gap of Dunlo
56 D. Flesch Bowl

PLATE 136

E. BROWN JR DEL.

LITH. BY N. CURRIER.

DIMENSIONS.

LENGTH OF KEEL .... 208 FEET.
LENGTH ON DECK .... 225 FEET
LENGTH OVERALL (FROM KNIGHT HEADS TO TAFFRAIL) 235 FEET

EXTREME BREADTH OF BEAM .... 41 FEET
DEPTH OF HOLD .... 21¼ FEET
TONNAGE PER REGISTER 1750
BUILT BY DONALD MᶜKAY AT EAST BOSTON MASS. 1851.

Entered according to Act of Congress, in the year 1852 by N Currier, in the Clerk's Office of the District Court of the Southern District of N.Y.

To Messrs Grinnell Minturn & Co This Print of their Splendid

CLIPPER SHIP "FLYING CLOUD".

is Respectfully dedicated by the Publisher

NEW YORK PUBLISHED BY N. CURRIER, 152 NASSAU STREET

PLATE 137

PUBLISHED BY CURRIER & IVES

THE CELEBRATED YACHT "AMERICA".

WINNER OF THE "QUEEN'S CUP", VALUE 100 GUINEAS.

In the Royal Yacht Squadron Match for all Nations at Cowes, England, Aug. 22, 1851.

115 NASSAU ST. NEW YORK

PLATE 138

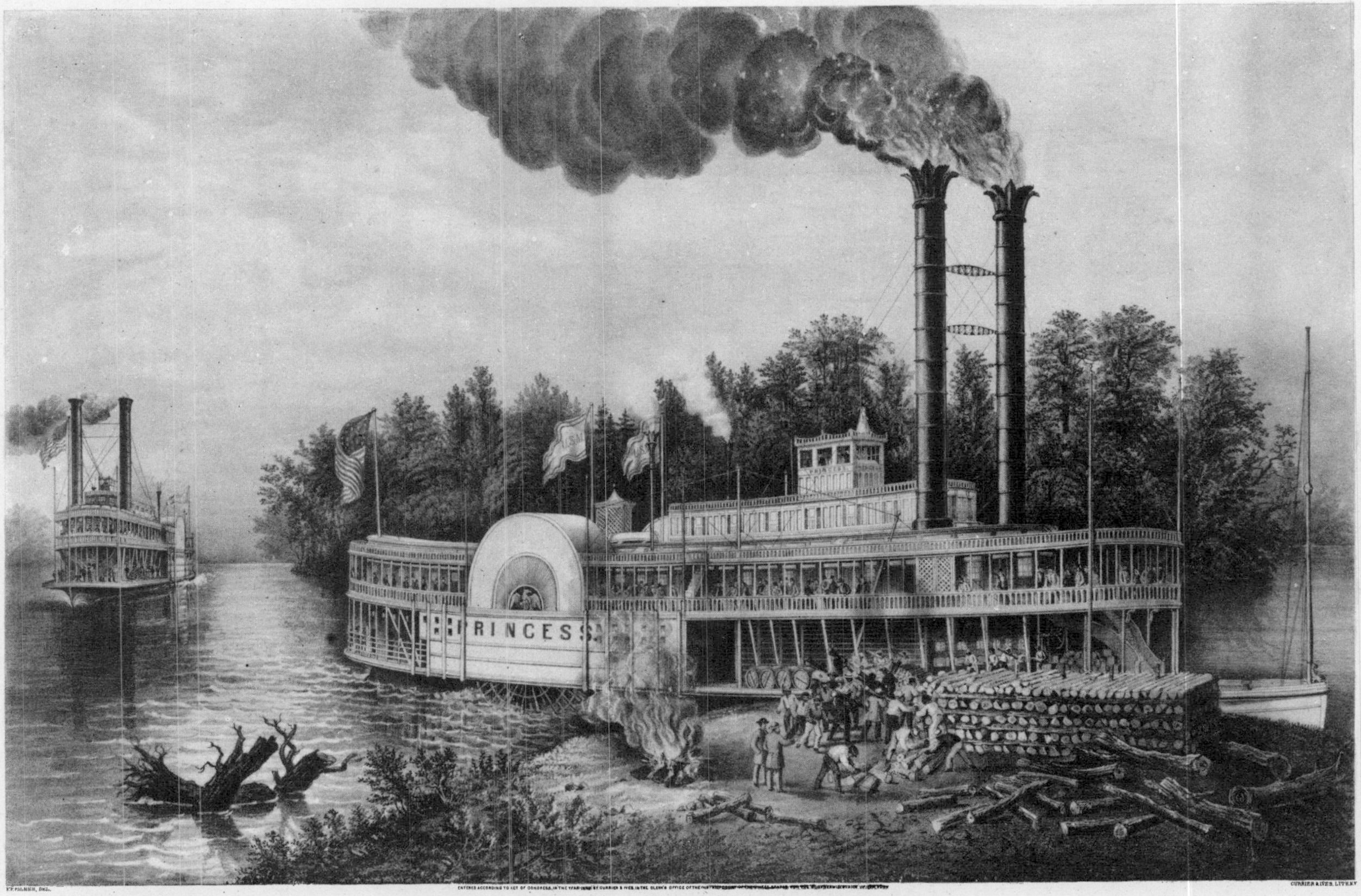

"WOODING UP" ON THE MISSISSIPPI.

PLATE 139

Published by Currier & Ives.   FORT JACKSON   Copyright. Amos Sweeney.   Entered according to Act of Congress in 1862 by Currier & Ives in the Clerks Office of the District Court for the Southern District of New York   FORT ST. PHILLIP.   152 NASSAU ST. NEW YORK.
Drawn from Nature & Master Plate.   Pensacola.   Mare Island, San california work at New York.   Oneida.   Richmond.   New York.   Mississippi. description retouch. Plate & drawing.
Brooklyn.   Varuna   Kineo

THE SPLENDID NAVAL TRIUMPH ON THE MISSISSIPPI, APRIL 24TH 1862.

DESTRUCTION OF THE REBEL GUNBOATS, RAMS AND IRON CLAD BATTERIES BY THE UNION FLEET UNDER FLAG OFFICER FARRAGUT

The Attack was commenced on the 18th of April and continued until the 25th resulting in the Capture of FORTS JACKSON ST PHILLIP LIVINGSTON PIKE and the CITY OF NEW ORLEANS as well as the destruction of all the enemys
Gunboats Rams Floating Batteries (iron clad) Fire Rafts Booms and Chains The enemy with their own hands destroying Cotton and Shipping valued at from eight to ten millions of dollars
The sixth of this night attack was awfully grand the River was lit up with blazing rafts filled with pine knots and the Ships seemed to be fighting literally amidst flames and smoke

PLATE 140

SUMMER SCENES IN NEW YORK HARBOR.

NEW YORK, PUBLISHED BY CURRIER & IVES, 152 NASSAU STREET.

PLATE 141

BEACH SNIPE SHOOTING.

PLATE 142

PUBLISHED BY CURRIER & IVES.   125 NASSAU ST. NEW YORK.

THE GREAT BLACK SEA LION.

The Monarch of the Artic Seas.

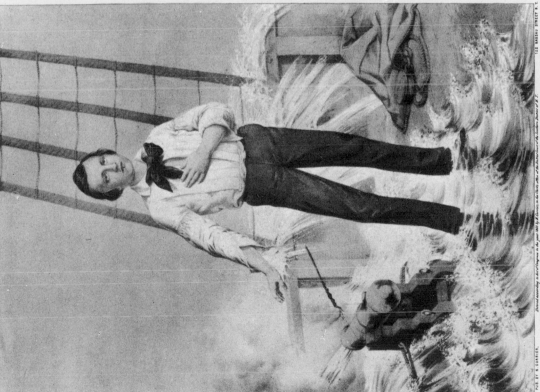

LITH. & PUB. BY N. CURRIER.   Entered according to Act of Congress in the year 1854 by N.Currier in the Clerks office of the District Court of the Southern District of N.Y.   152 NASSAU STREET N.Y.

THE LAST GUN OF THE ARCTIC.

STEWART HOLLAND
SEPT. 27TH 1854.

THE PORTRAIT FROM A DAGUERREOTYPE OF THE YOUNG HERO, IN POSSESSION OF HIS FATHER.

PLATE 143

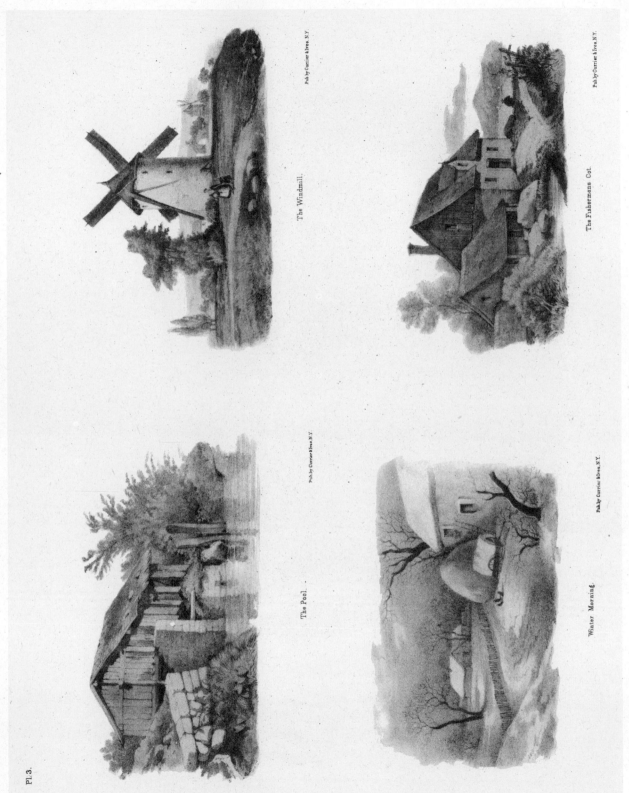

PL.3.

The Windmill.

Pub.by Currier & Ives, N.Y.

The Fishermans Cot.

Pub.by Currier & Ives, N.Y.

The Pool.

Pub.by Currier & Ives, N.Y.

Winter Morning.

Pub.by Currier & Ives, N.Y.

PLATE 144

TOM SAYERS CHAMPION OF ENGLAND.
Born at Pimlico, Brighton, Sussex 1826.
HEIGHT 5 FEET 8 INCHES. LOWEST FIGHTING WEIGHT 10 ST 10 LBS

Beat Aby Couch, March 19. 1849. £ 5 a side.
Beat Dan Collins, April 26. 1851. £ 25 a side.
Beat Jack Grant, Jan. 29. 1852. £ 100 a side.
Beat Jack Martin, Jan. 26. 1853. £ 100 a side.
Beaten by Nat Langham, Oct. 18. 1853. £ 100 a side.
Beat George Sims, Feb. 2. 1856. £ 50 a side.
Beat Harry Poulson, Jan. 29. 1856. £ 50 a side.

Beat Aaron Jones, Feb. 10. 1857. £ 100 a side.
Beat Wm. Perry, Slasher, June 16. 1857. £ 200 a side.
Beat Tom Paddock, June 16. 1858. £ 200 a side.
Beat Bill Benjamin, Apr. 5. 1859. £ 200 a side.
Beat Bob Brettle, Sep. 20. 1859. £ 200 a side.
Fought J.C. Heenan, 42 Rounds and drawn Apr. 17. 1860.

JOHN MORRISSEY,
Born February 5th. 1831.
HEIGHT 6 FEET. WEIGHT 170 LBS

Beat Thompson, Aug. 31. 1852. 11 Rounds 16 min.
$2000 a side.— Caledonia.
Beat Yankee Sullivan, Oct. 12. 1853. 37 Rounds 55 min.
$1000 a side.— Boston Corners N.Y.

Beat John C. Heenan,—"The Benicia Boy" Oct. 20.
1858. 11 Rounds, 22 min. $2500 a side.
Long Point Canada.

PLATE 145

LITH. & PUB. BY N. CURRIER,

DAYS PASSAGE OUT.
" " HOME.

Entered according to Act of Congress A.D. 1846 by N. Currier in the Clerks Office of the Dist Court of the South'n Dist of N. York

EXTRAORDINARY EXPRESS ACROSS THE ATLANTIC.

PILOT BOAT Wm J. ROMER, CAPT. M^c CUIRE.

LEAVING FOR ENGLAND — FEB. 9TH 1846

2 SPRUCE ST N.Y.

1ST MATE JOHN R. WILKIE.
2^D " JAMES CONNER.

PLATE 146

ROYAL MAIL STEAM SHIP,

ASIA.

Length over all		280 ft
Breadth of Beam		38 "
Breadth across Paddles		67 "
Depth of Hold		27 "

Diameter of Paddle		36 ft
Burthen per Register		2226 Tons
2 Engines 400 Horse Power each.		

PLATE 147

LITH. & PUB. BY N. CURRIER,   Entered according to Act of Congress in the year 1846 by N. Currier, in the Clerk's office of the District Court of the Southern District of N.Y.   2 Spruce St. Cor. of Spruce N.Y.

THE LOVERS WALK.

LITH. & PUB. BY N. CURRIER,   152 NASSAU ST. COR. OF SPRUCE N.Y.

THE MORNING RECREATION.

LITH. & PUB. BY N. CURRIER,   Entered according to Act of Congress in the year 1845 by N. Currier, in the Clerk's office of the District Court of the Southern District N.Y.   152 NASSAU ST. COR. OF SPRUCE N.Y.

BLACK EYED SUSAN.

Oh Susan! Susan! lovely dear,
My vows shall ever true remain,
Let me kiss off that falling tear,
We only part to meet again,
Change as ye list ye winds! my heart shall be
The faithful Compass, that still points to thee.

THE LITTLE MAMMA.

Lith. & Pub. by N. Currier, Nassau St. . . . . N.Y.

PLATE 148

SARA BERNHARDT.

NEW YORK PUBLISHED BY CURRIER & IVES 115 NASSAU ST.

Plate 149

CASTLE GARDEN · BEDLOES ISLAND · BERGEN POINT

UPPER AND LOWER BAY OF NEW YORK.

From the Battery looking South-west.

NEWPORT BEACH.

PLATE 150

THE STEAM SHIP PRESIDENT, (THE LARGEST IN THE WORLD) LIEUT. ROBERTS R.N. COMMANDER ON HER LAST VOYAGE FROM NEW YORK TO LIVERPOOL.

As last seen from the Packet Ship ORPHEUS, Capt. COLE in the terrific gale of March the 12th 1841 at 5 o'clock P. M. Lat. 39, 46 — Long. 71, bearing N. E. by E. by Compass steering East. —

In the inquiry before the British Consul, June the 5th 1841 — Capt. Cole of the Packet Ship Orpheus, stated that when he last saw the President on the 12th of March she was rising on the top of a tremendous sea pitching heavily and laboring tremendously — She was then situated in that dangerous part of the Atlantic Ocean: about midway between the Nantucket Shoal and the St. George's Banks, just where the Gulf Stream strikes soundings, and where the waves rise about straight up & down & as high as a four or five story house. And further that it was his belief that the President did not survive the gale, but foundered with all on board and that all perished before sundown on the 13th or in less than twenty four hours after he last saw her, most probably in the terrific night of March 12th 1841.

LOSS OF THE STEAMBOAT SWALLOW WHILE ON HER TRIP, FROM ALBANY TO NEW-YORK, on Monday Evening April 7th 1845. *When opposite Athens she struck a large rock, took fire broke in two and sunk — By which melancholy occurrence, it is supposed that nearly 40 lives were lost.*

Lith & Pub. by N. Currier 2 Spruce St N.Y.

PLATE 151

PLATE 152

LITH BY CURRIER & IVES, N.Y.　　　Entered according to Act of Congress in the Year 1852 by Currier & Ives in the Clerks Office of the Dist: Court of the South: Dist: of N.Y.

WASHINGTON'S DREAM.

New York, Published by CURRIER & IVES, 152 Nassau Street.

PLATE 152

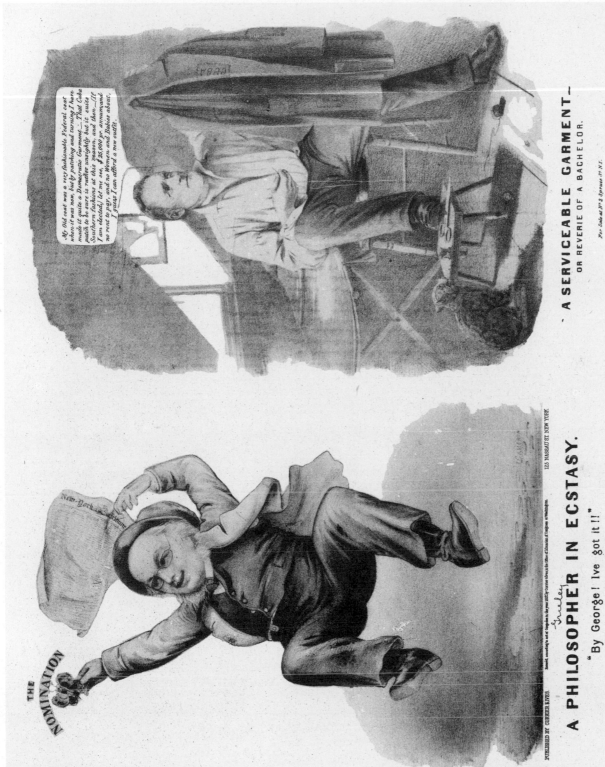

THE NOMINATION

PUBLISHED BY CURIER & IVES.   Entered according to act of Congress in the year 1872 by Currier & Ives in the office of Librarian of Congress at Washington.   125 NASSAU ST. NEW YORK

A PHILOSOPHER IN ECSTASY.

"By George! Ive got it!!"

'A SERVICEABLE GARMENT—
OR REVERIE OF A BACHELOR.

For Sale at N° 2 Spruce S.t N.Y.

PLATE 153

THE MODERN COLOSSUS.
EIGHTH WONDER OF THE WORLD.

THE PRESIDENTIAL FISHING PARTY OF 1848.

PLATE 154

THE GREAT REPUBLICAN REFORM PARTY,
Calling on their Candidate.
For Sale at No 2 Spruce St N.Y.

THE DEMOCRACY IN SEARCH OF A CANDIDATE.

Published by Currier & Ives, 152 Nassau St N.Y.

PLATE 155

THE CAPTURE OF AN UNPROTECTED FEMALE, OR THE CLOSE OF THE REBELLION.

226

CAVING IN, OR A REBEL "DEEPLY HUMILIATED".

Published by Currier & Ives, 152 Nassau St. N.Y.

PLATE 156

"THE IRREPRESSIBLE CONFLICT".
OR THE REPUBLICAN BARGE IN DANGER.

PROGRESSIVE DEMOCRACY_PROSPECT OF A SMASH UP.

Published by Currier & Ives, 152 Nassau St. N.Y.

PLATE 157

THE MAN OF WORDS, | THE MAN OF DEEDS,
WHICH DO YOU THINK THE COUNTRY NEEDS?

Published by Currier & Ives, 152 Nassau St N.Y.

RE-CONSTRUCTION,
OR "A WHITE MAN'S GOVERNMENT".

Published by Currier & Ives, 152 Nassau St. N.Y.

PLATE 158

GEORGE WASHINGTON.
First President of the United States.

Lith. & Pub. by N. Currier, 2 Spruce St. N.Y.

PLATE 159

A. Lincoln.

HON. ABRAHAM LINCOLN,

REPUBLICAN CANDIDATE FOR

SIXTEENTH PRESIDENT OF THE UNITED STATES.

Published by Currier & Ives, 152 Nassau St N.Y.

PLATE 160

RUNNING THE "MACHINE":

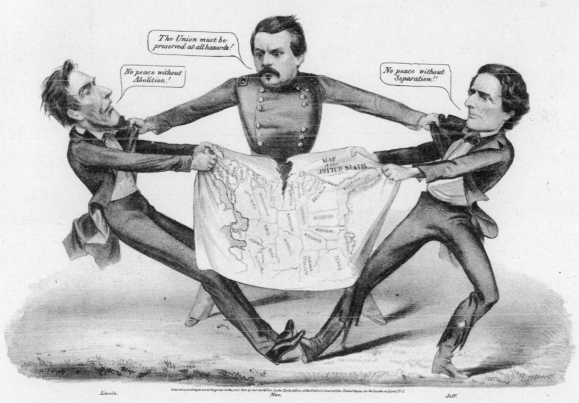

THE TRUE ISSUE OR "THATS WHATS THE MATTER".

PLATE 161

THE NATIONAL GAME. THREE "OUTS" AND ONE "RUN".
ABRAHAM WINNING THE BALL.

THE RAIL CANDIDATE.

PLATE 162

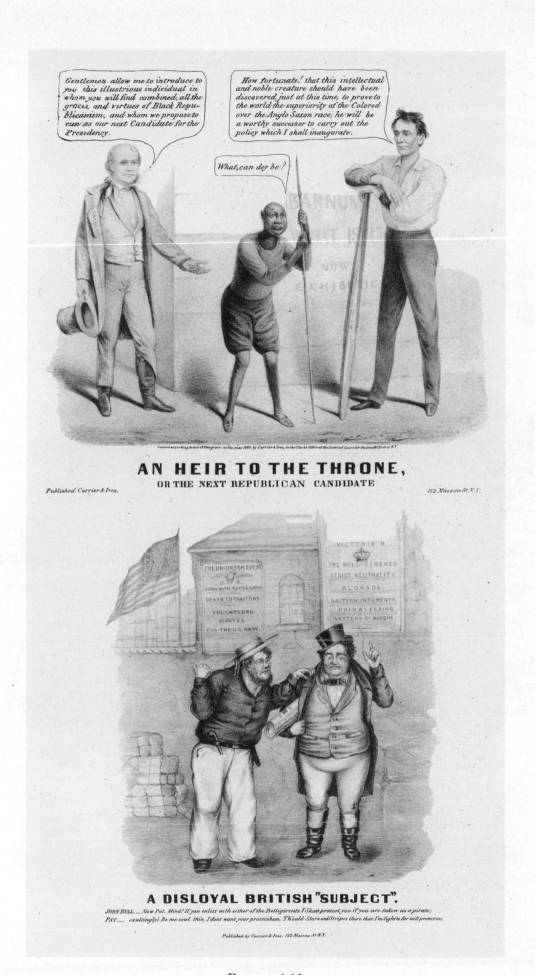

AN HEIR TO THE THRONE,
OR THE NEXT REPUBLICAN CANDIDATE

Published Currier & Ives, 152 Nassau St N.Y.

A DISLOYAL BRITISH "SUBJECT".

Plate 163

PUBLISHED BY CURRIER & IVES.

Entered according to Act of Congress, E.1869 by Currier & Ives, in the Clerks Office of the District Court of the United States, for the Southern District of New York.

152 NASSAU ST NEW YORK

THE AGE OF BRASS

or the triumphs of Womans rights

PLATE 164

MY CHILD! MY CHILD!

THEY'RE SAVED! THEY'RE SAVED!

PLATE 165

LAWRENCE, killed & wounded 83.   NIAGARA

PERRY'S VICTORY ON LAKE ERIE.
Fought Sept. 10th 1813.

This plate represents the position of the two Fleets at the moment when the NIAGARA is pushing through the enemy's line, pouring her thunder upon them from both broadsides, and forcing them to surrender in succession to the American Flag COMMODORE PERRY having a short time before left the LAWRENCE in a small boat, amidst a tremendous fire from the British Squadron and hoisted his Flag on board the NIAGARA

"We have met the enemy and they are ours." COM: O.H. PERRY.

Lith. & Pub. by N. Currier, 2 Spruce St. N.Y.

LITH. & PUB. BY N. CURRIER,   Entered according to Act of Congress in the year 1846 by N. Currier, in the Clerk's office of the District Court of the Southern District of N.Y.   2 SPRUCE ST. N.Y.

M'DONOUGH'S VICTY. ON LAKE CHAMPLAIN.

American Guns 86.		British Guns 95.
Loss 52 killed		Loss 84 killed
" 58 wounded		110 wounded

349

PLATE 166

'DARLING, I AM GROWING OLD—"

"T'WERE VAIN TO TELL THEE ALL I FEEL."
"What have you been eating and drinking?"
"Oh, Doctor, only Lobsters Cucumbers and Green Apples and Buttermilk."

PLATE 167

SUNNY SIDE.

THE RESIDENCE OF THE LATE WASHINGTON IRVING NEAR TARRYTOWN, N.Y.

THE MILL-DAM AT "SLEEPY HOLLOW".

PLATE 168

OUT FOR A DAYS SHOOTING.

Off for the Woods

PERMANENT FAIR GROUNDS OF THE

QUEENS COUNTY AGRICULTURAL SOCIETY.

MINEOLA, L. I.

Samuel T. Taber,
President.

John Harold,
Secretary.

LITHOGRAPHED & PUBLISHED FOR CHARLES R. BILL. 747 BROADWAY, N.Y.   The Grounds were laid out, and the Buildings designed by the Secretary.

PLATE 169

THE HOME OF THE DEER.

Morning in the Adirondacks

NEW YORK. PUBLISHED BY CURRIER & IVES 152 NASSAU STREET

SUNRISE ON LAKE SARANAC.

NEW YORK, PUBLISHED BY CURRIER & IVES, 152 NASSAU ST.

PLATE 170

PUBLISHED BY CURRIER & IVES   125 NASSAU ST NEW YORK

THE TROUT POOL.

BLACK BASS SPEARING,
ON THE RESTIGOUCHE. NEW BRUNSWICK.

NEW YORK. PUBLISHED BY CURRIER & IVES. 152 NASSAU St.

PLATE 171

VIEW OF NEW YORK.

FROM WEEHAWKEN—NORTH RIVER;

VIEW OF NEW YORK.

FROM BROOKLYN HEIGHTS.

PLATE 172

LADY SUFFOLK AND LADY MOSCOW.
HUNTING PARK COURSE, PHILA JUNE 18th 1850.
PURSE $250 MILE HEATS BEST 3 IN 5 TO SKELETON WAGONS.

Lady Suffolk. _____ 2. 1. 1. 1.
Lady Moscow. _____ 1. 2. 2. 2.
Time _____ 2.31 — 2.33 — 2.33 — 2.33.

GEORGE M. PATCHEN, BROWN DICK AND MILLERS DAMSEL.
IN THEIR SPLENDID TROTTING CONTEST FOR A PURSE OF $500.
OVER THE UNION COURSE L.I. JULY 7th 1860.
MILE HEATS BEST 3 IN 5 IN HARNESS.

D. TALLMAN ENTERED BR. S. GEO. M. PATCHEN _____ 1 1 2 2 1
D. PFIFER ENTERED B. G. BROWN DICK _____ 2 2 1 1 2
C. CARL ENTERED CH. M. MILLERS DAMSEL _____ 3 3 3 3 3
Time, 2.26½ — 2.26½ — 2.29 — 2.28½ — 2.29.

PLATE 173

STOCKS UP.

STOCKS DOWN.

PLATE 174

THE AMERICAN FIREMAN.
Always Ready.

NEW YORK, PUB'D BY CURRIER & IVES, 152 NASSAU ST.

PLATE 175

A BARE CHANCE.

A "LIMITED EXPRESS."
"Five seconds for Refreshments"!

PLATE 176

Lincoln.   Hamilton: Lafayette. Washington.   Cornwallis. Tarleton. O'Hara. Chewton.

SURRENDER OF CORNWALLIS,
AT YORK-TOWN Vᵃ· OCT· 1781.

Lith. & Pub. by N· Currier, 2 Spruce St. N. Y.

Entered according to Act of Congress in the year 1845 by N. Currier, in the Clerk's office of the District Court of the Southern District of N. Y.

PLATE 177

152 NASSAU ST NEW YORK

THE GREAT INTERNATIONAL BOAT RACE AUG. 27TH. 1869

BETWEEN OXFORD AND HARVARD ON THE RIVER THAMES NEAR LONDON 4 MILES 2 FURLONGS

Won by the Oxfords by a half length clear water. Time 22 Min. 20¾ Sec.

125 NASSAU ST NEW YORK

ICE-BOAT RACE ON THE HUDSON.

PLATE 178

BIRDS EYE VIEW OF
Mt. VERNON,
THE HOME OF WASHINGTON.

VIEW OF HARPERS FERRY, Va
(FROM THE POTOMAC SIDE.)

PLATE 179

LANDING OF THE PILGRIMS AT PLYMOUTH 11th DEC.1820.

Lith. & Pub by N Currier, 2 Spruce St N.Y.

THE DECLARATION OF INDEPENDENCE.

JULY 4th 1776.

PLATE 180

PUB? BY CURRIER & IVES.   Entered according to Act of Congress A? 1865 by Currier & Ives in the Clerks Office of the District Court of the United States for the Southern District of New York.   152 NASSAU ST. NEW YORK.

THE STORY OF THE FIGHT.

Twas there amid the storm of fire of shot and bursting shell,
Upon the ramparts bloody slope, our standard bearer fell,
But as in death his eye grew dim, one look on mys he cast,
Which nerved my arm & thrilled my heart as with a trumpet blast,
And forth I sprang and seized the Flag, and up the steep I bore
And planted it in triumph, there amid the battle's roar

Around me gleamed the clashing steel, I felt the deadly thrust,
But down the rebel ensign tore, and tramp'd it in the dust,
I saw my comrades pressing on, and heard their rallying cry,
I heard their glad victorious shout, and saw the foemen fly,
A moment more and sound and sight were fading fast away,
Bleeding and senseless on the ground beneath the flag I lay.

Entered according to Act of Congress A? 1862 by Currier & Ives under Clerks Office of the District Court for the Southern District of NY   LITH. BY CURRIER & IVES.

LIFE IN THE CAMP.

Preparing for Supper

PLATE 181

LITH. & PUB. BY N. CURRIER.

2 Oscillating Engines of
500 Horse power (nominally)
Diameter of cylinders . . . . 82¼ inches.
Length of Stroke . . . . 6 feet.

152 NASSAU ST. COR. OF SPRUCE, N.Y.

Length over all . . . . 300 feet.
Beam . . . . 51 feet 6 inches.
Depth from promenade deck . . . . 40 feet 10½ inches.
Capacity for cargo, about . . . . 3000 tons.
Ditto for coals . . . . 1200 tons.

THE IRON STEAM SHIP GREAT BRITAIN.
OFF SANDY HOOK MAY·14TH 1852.

354

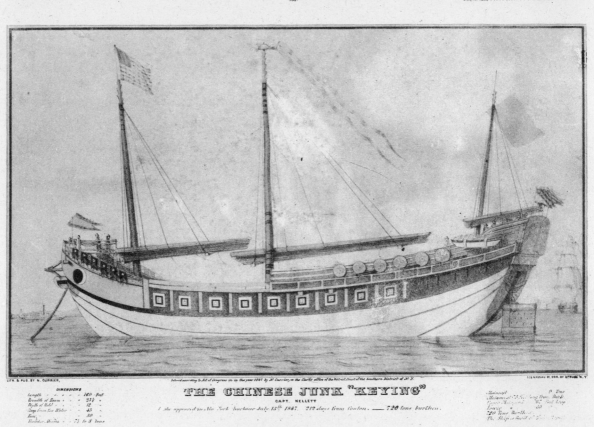

LITH. & PUB. BY N. CURRIER.

Entered according to Act of Congress in in the year 1847 by N. Currier, in the Clerks office of the District court of the Southern District of N.Y.

152 NASSAU ST. COR. OF SPRUCE, N.Y.

DIMENSIONS

Length · · · · · 160 feet
Breadth of Beam · · · · 25½ feet
Depth of Hold · · · · 12
Deep from the Water · · · 43
Bow · · · · 30
Rudder, Weighs · · · 7½ to 8 tons

Mainmast · · · · 9 Tons
Mainmast 7½ feet long from Deck
Foremast Main mast 85 feet long
Davos · · · did
70 Tons Burthen
The Ship is built of . . .

THE CHINESE JUNK "KEYING"
CAPT. KELLETT

I she appeared in New York harbour July 15th 1847.   212 days from Canton.   720 tons burthen.

PLATE 182

BRER THULDY'S STATUE
LIBERTY FRIGHTENIN DE WORLD.
To be stuck up on Bedbugs Island - Jarsey Flats, opposit de United States.

(Only Authorized Edition.)

THE ÆSTHETIC CRAZE.

What's de matter wid de Nigga ? Why Oscar you's gone wild !

ON HIS STYLE.
"Take a mity smart lokymoky to kotch dis coon!"

OFF HIS NUT.
"Gracious Massy, I'se struck de comet!"

PLATE 183

PUBLISHED BY CURRIER & IVES   115 NASSAU ST. NEW YORK

LEXINGTON.

THE GREAT MONARCH OF THE TURF AND SIRE OF RACERS.

BY BOSTON OUT OF ALICE GARNEAL.

Winner of the great 4 mile heat race against Lecompte's time 7:26 for $20,000, over the Metairie Course, New Orleans, April 2nd 1855.

Time   7 : 19 ¾.

PUBLISHED BY CURRIER & IVES   COPYRIGHT 1880, BY CURRIER & IVES, N.Y.   115 NASSAU ST. NEW YORK

IMPORTED MESSENGER.

THE GREAT FOUNTAIN HEAD - IN AMERICA - OF "THE MESSENGER BLOOD."

Foaled 1780 got by Mambrino, he by Engineer, he by Sampson, he by Blaze, he by Flying Childers, he by the famous
Darley Arabian. Messenger's Dam was by Turf, he by Matchem, he by Cade, he by the great
Godolphin Arabian, and the sire of the Dam of Messenger's Dam was also by the Godolphin Arabian.

PLATE 184

WASHINGTON TAKING LEAVE OF THE OFFICERS OF HIS ARMY,

AT FRANCIS'S TAVERN, BROAD STREET, NEW YORK, DEC? 4TH 1783.

"With a heart full of love and gratitude, I now take leave of you. I most devoutly wish that your latter days may be as prosperous and happy, as your former ones have been glorious and honorable."

GENERAL FRANCIS MARION, OF SOUTH CAROLINA.

In his swamp Encampment, inviting a British Officer to share his Dinner of sweet Potatoes and cold Water.

PLATE 185

THE WAY THEY COME FROM CALIFORNIA.

THE GREAT EXHIBITION OF 1851.
AMERICAN DEPARTMENT.

PLATE 186

A SUMMER RAMBLE.

NEW YORK, PUB? BY CURRIER & IVES, 152 NASSAU ST.

PLATE 187

PUBLISHED BY CURRIER & IVES

ENTERED ACCORDING TO ACT OF CONGRESS IN THE YEAR 1870, BY CURRIER & IVES IN THE CLERKS OFFICE, IN THE DISTRICT COURT OF THE UNITED STATES FOR THE SOUTHERN DISTRICT OF NEW YORK

152 NASSAU ST. NEW YORK

THE EXPRESS TRAIN

LITH. & PUB. BY N. CURRIER.

152 NASSAU ST. COR. OF SPRUCE N.Y.

THE EXPRESS TRAIN.

127

PLATE 188

BUFFALO BULL, CHASING BACK.

"TURN ABOUT IS FAIR PLAY".

NEW YORK, PUBᴰ BY CURRIER & IVES, 152 NASSAU ST

THE SNOW-SHOE DANCE.

TO THANK THE GREAT SPIRIT FOR THE FIRST APPEARANCE OF SNOW.

NEW YORK, PUBᴰ BY CURRIER & IVES, 152 NASSAU ST

PLATE 189

PUBLISHED BY CURRIER & IVES   125 NASSAU ST. NEW YORK

AMERICAN WHALERS CRUSHED IN THE ICE.
"BURNING THE WRECKS TO AVOID DANGER TO OTHER VESSELS"

PUBLISHED BY CURRIER & IVES   125 NASSAU ST. NEW YORK

THE HOME OF THE SEAL.

PLATE 190

HOLIDAYS IN THE COUNTRY.

TROUBLESOME FLIES.

New York Published by Currier & Ives, 152 Nassau St.

The old Barn Floor

PLATE 191

THE TRIAL OF PATIENCE.

NEW YORK, PUBLISHED BY CURRIER & IVES, 152 NASSAU STREET.

AN INCREASE OF FAMILY.

NEW YORK, PUBLISHED BY CURRIER & IVES, 152 NASSAU ST.

PLATE 192